The **HOW** of

A GUIDE TO GIVING A SPEECH THAT WILL POSITIVELY BLOW 'EM AWAY

TONY CARLSON

AMACOM
American Management Association
NEW YORK • ATLANTA • BRUSSELS • CHICAGO • MEXICO CITY • SAN FRANCISCO
SHANGHAI • TOKYO • TORONTO • WASHINGTON, D. C.

Special discounts on bulk quantities of AMACOM books are available to corporations, professional associations, and other organizations. For details, contact Special Sales Department, AMACOM, a division of American Management Association, 1601 Broadway, New York, NY 10019.
Tel.: 212-903-8316. Fax: 212-903-8083.
Web site: www.amacombooks.org

This publication is designed to provide accurate and authoritative information in regard to the subject matter covered. It is sold with the understanding that the publisher is not engaged in rendering legal, accounting, or other professional service. If legal advice or other expert assistance is required, the services of a competent professional person should be sought.

Library of Congress Cataloging-in-Publication Data

Carlson, Tony.
        The how of WOW : a guide to giving a speech that will positively blow 'em away / Tony Carlson.
            p.   cm.
        Includes bibliographical references and index.
        ISBN-10: 0-8144-7251-6
        ISBN-13: 978-0-8144-7251-4
        1. Public speaking.   2. Communication in management.   I. Title.

    PN4193.B8C37   2005
    808.5'1—dc22

                                                            2004022112

Printing number

10 9 8 7 6 5 4 3

Contents

Acknowledgments

In the general chatter after a major speech given by a client of mine once, a person who had liked the speech came up to me, knowing that I had written it.

"Great stuff. Tell me, how long did it take to write that speech?"

For once in my life, I had the right riposte ready.

"All my life," I said. And I was serious.

Writers draw something from everyone with whom they come in contact, every article they read, movie they see, experience they have. It's common to think that of creative artists, poets, and fiction writers. But it is also true of the best commercial writers, for the stories they tell are a distillation of the stories they have heard, read, and seen, winnowed to the core, shined up and polished and presented again, like new. It's nicer to say that than to think that we just steal material willy-nilly.

It's in that context that I say that all of this work is mine and mine alone. So any errors are mine and mine alone.

That is not to say I didn't receive tremendous support from a wide range of people in the conception and birth of this book, and the speeches to which I refer in it.

At the head of that list is clearly my family, not only for their encouragement—cattle prods were occasionally necessary—and patience—"Quiet, kids, Dad's working on his book again . . .

still!"—but also for providing such a rich source of stories and anecdotes, which I shamelessly exploit to bring some color to the presentation palette of my clients.

My wife, Donna, and children, Katie and Jenny, are more a part of this book than they'll ever know. As is my late father, Don, who first told me about setting up a straw man in a speech more than 30 years ago, my mother, Madeline, whose fierce Irish pride and love supports all the dreamers in her extended family, and my brother, Gus, who cleared the path in the publishing world for me.

There is also much in this book inspired by a small number of executives who over the years have had faith in my advice even when lawyers and some PR greyhairs were counseling otherwise. At the top of this group is Bob Ferchat, who began as a boss but opened his mind to me as a mentor and his heart to me as a friend.

Without question, I want to thank Ellen Kadin, who as an editor used just the right amount of carrot and stick to get this project out of my mind and onto the page.

I have imposed on the time and goodwill of all these people and many more. And now I have the cheek to ask to impose on yours. You may not like what I have to say. You may not agree with all or any of it. But you have only mediocrity to lose. And an audience full of wows to gain.

Tony Carlson

The How of WOW

Prologue: Rising Above the Crowd

Every working day in North America, more than 10,000 people get up on their hind legs and deliver speeches. Twenty-five minutes later, 9,998 are forgotten by everyone except perhaps the speechgiver, the writer, and the speechgiver's subordinates. Such a sound and fury signifying nothing. A pebble dropped into the Marianas Trench leaves as lasting an impression.

So what. The audience eats a passable, if lukewarm, meal. Downs a glass of house wine. Groans at a bad joke and toddles off back to work or to the next conference session. As mildly diverting as another rerun of *Friends*, and infinitely less painful than a colonoscopy. Everybody's happy, right?

Really? Consider this.

Estimates vary, but some observers figure the conference business in the United States alone is worth $120 billion a year. That's a lot of the long green being snoozed away by people bored by bizspeak and blinded by punchless PowerPoint.

I can hear what you're thinking. That the real work of conferences doesn't go on during the speeches and panel sessions. It

1

happens in the corridors and over dinners and in the hotel rooms. That's where the deals are hatched and consummated. That's where the value lies. Maybe.

The Bland Leading the Bland

But hundreds of thousands of people still sit through the parade of mediocrity that inhabits platforms across the land. We in the audience are often bored, itching to get to the real business—or pleasure—just over the horizon of the next keynote yawn.

You have to ask why. And the answer, most times, is because that's the way it has always been. With few exceptions, public speeches—especially by business leaders—have been allowed to become the elevator music of the communications world. They barely impinge on conscious thought. Pleasant enough, but would you really miss them if they weren't there?

What a waste, in so many ways.

It's not that the speakers or the writers or the graphic artists are dumb. Many are highly competent, even brilliant, at what they do. Yet they opt for the safe harbor of formulaic style and substance. Conventional wisdom rules; edgy ideas are few and far between. They state and restate the obvious.

But truth be told, boring speeches were the rule long before anyone had heard of Enron. My theory: People don't understand what a powerful tool they have at their disposal when they're on the podium. Public speaking is such an ingrained fear in so many of us that we just want to get it over and done with. Why prolong the ordeal? If you pay little attention to it, maybe you can avoid sleepless nights or, worse, those awful dreams where you walk to the microphone only to remember you're still in your pajamas . . . or less.

Allowing Mediocrity

Then, too, many speakers depend on a docile audience, all too willing to yawn through the monotony, aiding and abetting a let's-get-it-over-with approach. Or making allowances in sympathy for the poor devil whose number has come up and who has to actually give the speech.

It's a wonder why audiences don't expect—and demand—more for their money, even if it is the virtually weightless expense account kind of currency.

It's a wonder they let speakers get away with pointing to a slide and saying: "As you can see here [when they really can't see anything if they're more than four rows from the front], thanks to our rigorous focus on managing capital inputs and operational expenses and on driving high-margin product lines, our EBITDA growth jumped almost half a percent, to 4.35 percent in Q2 of this year, compared to the similar period for last year, a stark contrast to the negative growth [negative GROWTH?] we experienced in the 'Perfect Storm' that hit the high-tech sector in the two years prior . . . zzzzzzzzzzzzzzzzzzz."

But it's not just the money. Bill Jensen, the principal of the New Jersey–based Jensen Group leadership consultancy, tells his audiences the single most important number in business is 1,444.[1] That's the number of minutes in a day. The number of minutes each of us has to spend. A number that remains constant regardless of the state of the economy, world peace, or the Mets' bullpen. It's a nonrenewable resource that we cannot afford to waste.

Think how grateful an audience would be if the speaker respected the importance of their time by delivering some real insight, if not enlightenment. Some meaning where once was only data. If the speaker offered fewer platitudes but more attitude.

Sought to elicit more of the "I've never thought of it that way" kind of response. Less of the "been there, heard that" déjà vu.

Insight. Enlightenment. Meaning. Stimulation. Wit. Entertainment.

That's what I look for when I open a magazine or a book or a Web site. It's what I crave when I fork over $14 for a movie, or $90 a month for digital television, cable, or satellite. Should a speaker expect to make an impact, be memorable, if he or she delivers less?

Yet that is what so often happens. This powerful tool of communication is devolving into a kind of beige wallpaper, inoffensive to anyone to be sure, but ultimately forgettable. And probably before the audience returns to their cubicles back at the office.

Question is, what shall we do about it?

Over the last 20 years, I have had the opportunity to see thousands of people give speeches and presentations. I've written hundreds more. I struggle to remember even a Homer-Simpson handful of them, even those that arose from my own fevered keyboard.

More often than not, I've been underwhelmed by the sameness, depressed by the knowledge that there's another 20 minutes of my life I've spent with no return on the investment—and no chance of getting them back.

Yet I have also had the privilege to work with a number of senior executives who frequented the speaking platforms of a wide variety of venues, from academic and business conferences to parliamentary and congressional hearings. In that work—thanks to some insightful and even courageous individuals who actually agreed to speak the words I put in their mouths—we occasionally broke through the swamp of mediocrity, homogeneity, and just plan dullness that afflicts the majority of speeches today.

We started with the notion that anytime one is asked to get up to speak formally, it is an opportunity, not something to be got through. It is an opportunity not only for the organization the speaker represents, but also—and probably more important—a virtual *carte blanche* for the speaker to take the bushel basket off his or her own light.

Not all of these speakers were comfortable with public speaking—few people are. But the best of them rose above the personal ordeal of standing intellectually naked in front of often-critical strangers because they understood what they had to gain by being memorable.

In an Internet-driven world, where the flood of available information is rising at an unprecedented rate, where graphics and streaming video add vivid new dimensions to often dry data, it's getting even tougher to be memorable when you stand up in front of a live audience.

But it can be done. And that's what this book is about.

About This Book

Part I addresses the most important question: what's in it for you, as a speaker. Why should you care about being memorable on the podium in the first place. And it sets the stage for breaking through the noise to really connect with your audience. Part II looks at that critical period between receiving the invitation and getting down to the actual writing. In Part III, we look at the ongoing preparation you need to do to really excel on the podium, and cover five ways to connect with the audience from the first moments at the microphone. Part IV tackles the nuts and bolts of the speech—how to give shape and substance to your subject and then express yourself in clear, impactful language. After the writing is done, it's time to deliver, and that's what Part V covers: from preparation of the delivery copy to establishing a memorable persona on the dais. Finally, Part V also looks at one of the most sadly neglected areas of speechmaking: what to do after the talking is done, with ideas to market and repackage the material to make the most of your investment in it.

In the end, this book is not about getting the data right. It's not about delivering messages. It's not about overcoming stage fright.

It's about connecting with a live audience, from the moment you hear about the speaking opportunity until long after the applause has long died down.

You'll learn, for instance, why the traditional model for speeches is a road map to forgettability. And why slides and videos are, at best, the most overrated gimmicks since the push-button transmission in the 1957 Plymouth Fury.

I am under no illusion that this book covers every possible strategy for you to stand out on the platform. I am also well aware that not all of the suggestions and guidelines offered here are applicable all the time for every speaker.

My hope for you is that after reading this book, you will understand the dynamic that exists in and around the speech-giving process, you will see the benefits of standing out on the platform, and you'll be more insistent that you do just that when the opportunity arises.

Give the audience a memory. Make them say, "Wow!"

Note

1. From a presentation to Bell Canada by Bill Jensen, CEO, The Jensen Group. Morristown, NJ. August 27, 2003.

PART I

Why Should You Care?

Glory is fleeting but obscurity is forever.

—NAPOLEON BONAPARTE

Take Off the Bushel Basket

Proposition: Most speeches are dull, forgettable.

Response: So what? Why should we care?

It's not hard to imagine a busy executive's rebuttal: Giving speeches is really low on my list of priorities when I have more empowered board members looking over my shoulder, not to mention the SEC and other enforcement agencies, and customers whose expectations are becoming more and more demanding (i.e. unrealistic). So what if I fulfill my obligation and fill 20 minutes or half an hour or even an hour with some slides and numbers . . . yes, numbers are always good. It's not brain surgery—no one dies.

True. But since when has settling for good enough ever been a winning strategy? And, depending on your point of view, there are some pretty interesting answers to "So what?"

Building the Personal Brand

There's really only one place to begin when talking about points of view—with yourself. What's in it for you to take a risk, to stand out from the safe crowd on the podium? Egocentric? Maybe. But human nature. And after all, there aren't too many Albert Schweitzers around.

What's in it for you? The answer is simple: Delivering memorable speeches and presentations is a powerful tool to build your own personal brand. You can "make your name" by working on your presentation skills. And if you have ambitions of succeeding to the senior levels of any organization—public or private sector—you need a name people know . . . and respect.

And that depends on approaching the preparation and delivery of a speech not as an obligation but as an opportunity. There you are, the last speaker on the last panel of the day. Just one person stands between the audience and the bar: you. Or you're the last-minute guest at the monthly Kiwanis supper and business meeting. The temptation to get in and get out as quickly and quietly as possible is strong. But even in these instances—perhaps especially in these instances—you have a chance to show what you're made of, as an expert in your field and just as important, as a person.

On a beige canvas, even a dash of color makes an impact, becomes memorable. If I'm asked to speak, and I've got a few dozen (or hundred) captive souls in a room, and no one's talking except me, I can be that color. I can be memorable.

Am I going to get a better chance to show what I can do? Not often.

Same thing in the boardroom or sales presentations or service club luncheons. All chances to stand out.

This is not the time to say to ourselves, well, if we can get through the 20 minutes without fainting or otherwise embarrassing ourselves, mission accomplished.

Woody Allen was just kidding when he said 80 percent of life is just showing up. Did Columbus turn back after he saw land, or did he come ashore? We don't remember Neil Armstrong for circling the moon—although he did. We remember him for landing.

When else do you have the floor? When else can you make your colleagues envious, your bosses take notice, and your audience see you and your cause in an entirely new—and radiant—light?

What makes a good speaker also makes a very promotable individual. People often pay only lip service to the importance of communications skills, especially in organizations dominated by engineers or other technical disciplines. But the fact is that any organization is essentially a human enterprise. And the communication between and among those humans is both the glue that holds it together and the fuel that drives innovation and growth.

It's what the patron saint of management, Peter Drucker, was getting at when he called management a social function and a liberal art. "Management is about human beings. . . . Every enterprise is composed of people with different skills and knowledge doing many different kinds of work. It must be built on communication and on individual responsibility."[1]

Communication and individual responsibility. Two concepts that come together on the platform in the person of the speaker who demonstrates, in real time, his or her personal commitment. They are made real through the words and ideas in the speaker's mouth. And just as important, in the implicit messages that flow from the willingness to stand up and do something that is in the top three of things people hate to do—speak in front of a crowd.

One still has to be able to deliver all the other goods that executives need: financial, technical, sales skills, whatever. But you also must make sure other people know you can do all that stuff, especially people beyond your immediate circle of influence. And that means building a personal brand.

In turn, that means demonstrating that great intangible: leadership. Senior executives, no matter the organization, not only must be capable in their craft, but must also have the courage to lead. For it does take courage. Leadership is not about maintaining the status quo. It is about going into uncharted territory in pursuit of a well-articulated view of life. It is about having, as Colin Powell has said, the willingness to piss people off. To ask the unaskable question. To voice the unpopular idea.

It takes courage just to get up and talk in front of people. Doing it well, taking the audience places they haven't been, takes even more. But the rewards are worth it.

And ask yourself this: How tough can it be? Given the wasteland of dullness on daises from coast to coast to coast, it's not that big a stretch to think that you might make an enormous impact. In the company of Munchkins, even Tom Cruise looks tall. Someone who really knows what to do can seem to be a giant, and use that to establish a personal brand that translates into an entirely new level of success.

All it takes is the mind-set to see the opportunity, the will to go after it, and some understanding of what makes a speech work. Because good ones—as rare as they may be—do.

Bland Does Nothing for Brand

Of course, there are other answers to the what's-in-it-for-you question, important reasons to want to be memorable beyond building your personal brand.

Think about what your speeches mean to your organization's brand, a mission-critical element of business in today's increasingly commoditized world.

First, it's clear that, in the wake of the dot-gones, consumers of all sorts are placing more confidence in trusted brands. As hundreds of upstart companies failed in the first three years of this century, whether because of unrealistic business plans or plain and simple crooked accounting, people searched for companies that had stood the test of time and had the resources to be around for another long period. So today, like never before, brand is a critical success driver.

Without going through Marketing 101, it's common knowledge that Brand with an uppercase B is composed of a variety of inputs. Price is one. Just ask Wal-Mart how it got to be the world's largest company. Penetration is another: There may be a Target or a K-Mart in every town, but you have to look a little harder for a Bloomingdales or Saks Fifth Avenue. And once you find it, you're willing to pay more than you would at the Filene's around the corner. Go figure.

But a large element—perhaps the most important element of brand—is emotional, that connection the customer, or potential customer, or former customer makes with the idea of your organization.

I had a great experience with my first Honda Civic and have been loyal ever since, not just for the quality of the product but for the nonlogical connection I made with the company—an upstart in North America at the time, a producer of environmentally friendly gas misers good for getting from point A to point B and not much else.

Conversely, my wife and I had nothing but trouble with a used Aspen station wagon we bought when the kids came along. The brand name conjured up visions of carefree times at an upscale mountain resort, or a beautiful tree whose silver-backed leaves define summer along many a rural laneway. The reality of our Aspen wagon: not so much. Obviously, it was just one lemon among how many thousands of good Dodge cars. But it planted a negative brand association and influenced my car-buying decisions ever since.

That's why organizations pay so much attention to every aspect of their business as it is seen by customers. Customer service reps are trained incessantly. Every word of ad copy, every color in the illustration or backdrop in the TV commercial, every model's expression, ethnicity, and demeanor are ruthlessly pored over.

The look and feel of brochures, the look and location of offices and stores, the look and lifespan of the logo, are all intensely scrutinized because marketeers know that each element has the potential to build, or undermine, the all-important brand.

By contrast, speakers and speeches fly out the door after relatively cursory consideration. The speaker pays attention, of course. Maybe a writer if the speaker is senior enough. A senior PR person and a couple of subject matter experts, the VPs and managers who know how many widgets the company can churn out in a 24-hour period.

Don't get me wrong. There's lots of effort, lots of busy work and heavy sighs as people shuffle clichés about. But more often than not, the unspoken premise is, how do we get through this without creating trouble? How do we fulfill the obligation and still stay under the radar?

Where's the logic in that?

The fact is that the speaker, any speaker, is the organization's brand incarnate. He or she is going to affect brand awareness, just by showing up. But he or she can choose, subconsciously or not, between enhancing the image—albeit by tiny steps in all likelihood—or poking a hole in the balloon. And frankly, like an automotive lemon, a bad speech can sour an audience on a brand a lot faster than a great one can build loyalty.

But surely, the skeptical executive asks, one speech here or there isn't going to make a difference to my brand. We spend $18 gazillion every year on the most sophisticated advertising.

Well, that's what the ad agencies want you to believe, anyway. Not that they have too much of a vested interest in driving up their billings. But I digress.

There is a growing body of evidence that what really builds

brand is not advertising but public relations—of which speech-making is a critical tool.

In their recent book, *The Fall of Advertising & the Rise of PR*,[2] Al and Laura Ries point out that advertising, because it's bought and paid for, lacks credibility, the crucial ingredient of brand building. In case after case, the authors document companies that spent millions of dollars on advertising with no discernible impact, except negative, to their bottom line or market share. They argue that there is too much advertising today for any of it to be memorable. And more fundamentally, they suggest that people are sophisticated enough to understand that ads are all one-sided and don't tell the whole story.

"Microsoft reportedly spent $1 billion in advertising for the worldwide launch of Windows XP," they wrote in one instance. "But what will motivate prospects to switch from Windows 98, Windows Me, or Windows 2000 to Windows XP? Certainly not what they read in the advertising. They will make their decisions based on the thousands of publicity stories that have run in the media."[3]

And, I would submit, on people's perception of Bill Gates and his lieutenants, gleaned from media stories and the endless round of in-person speeches they make. A few months ago, I was whisked breathlessly (my host, not me) to Breakfast with Bill, an intimate affair in which my host and I, and another 1,498 people, gathered in a cavernous convention center room like acolytes looking for loaves and fishes. We each received a T-shirt, squeezed into a capsule not much larger than a tube of lip balm. "I had breakfast with Bill Gates" it read, reinforcing the brand and the message every time we put the thing on to mow the lawn. That aside, whether we were a fan or not, here was a chance to see the richest man in the world, the leader of this incredible venture, and assess him on a very human level. He was, in that appearance, in that moment, the brand itself. Larger than life in some ways but also, clearly, one of us, for it sure looked like he puts his pants on one leg at a time.

It's the same brand personification, although to a far lesser extent, for any speaker from any organization. What the audience is seeing in the speaker, what they're getting to know and judge in a particularly personal way, is the organization itself. What sort of organization is it that would put this person in a position of influence, that would feel comfortable having this person speak for it? For these appearances, for those moments, the speaker *is* the brand.

That's why mediocrity should never be acceptable. That's why every aspect of an appearance should get the same attention as the design of a store, or the thrust of an ad campaign. The speaker's dress, haircut, arm gestures, are all important because they will form immediate associations for the audience with the speaker and the organization. Where the speaker appears on the agenda says something about the clout of the organization. Whether the speaker reads notes or talks to slides or just tells stories . . . all these go to the executive's command of the subject, of course, but also to his or her knowledge of the organization and the issues it faces. Credibility, in other words.

It's not rocket science. When you see a speaker who looks right for the job, whatever that look might be, who stimulates your mind, someone with whom you wouldn't mind sitting down to coffee, you are at least a little predisposed to look twice at the organization he or she represents. You've made a connection with the brand.

But you're not going to make that connection with a speaker who achieves mediocrity, who does not stand out from the pack on the podium. And for those in the pack, they've just wasted your time and money, as well as their own. They might as well not have bothered.

Restoring Confidence

This brand-building potential of a memorable speech extends beyond the speaker's organization. Today, business, especially big business, is overdrawn on its public confidence account thanks to the hysterical, tail-chasing market optimism of the dotcom period and, more important, the shenanigans of the leaders at companies such as Enron, WorldCom, Andersen, Adelphia . . . and, well, to our shame the list goes on, doesn't it, Martha?

In this time of soul searching, there is an urgent need to restore trust in the species known as the business leader, understanding that what one can lose overnight cannot be restored in the same time frame. Only by aggressively addressing the issues of trust will corporations regain the flexibility and freedom they need to attract the resources necessary to serve their customers and shareholders.

And that means many small trust-building actions.

The question is, where do speeches fit, given that a speech, by definition, is all talk and no action?

Good question, but it sells short the impact that a person standing up in front of a roomful of strangers can have simply by making a public commitment, and reinforcing over and over again how he or she—and the organization—are living up to the promise.

What happens in an effective, memorable speech is primarily a connection between the speaker and the audience, a connection on a fundamentally human level. It is not about statistics, or anecdotes, but about the implicit contract between speaker and audience: "This is the truth as I know it, these are the issues as I perceive them, and this is what I propose to do about it," the speaker says. If the speaker is good, the argument sound, the approach credible, the audience will reply with a collective "We believe you." Or at least "We'll wait and see." If the speaker prevaricates, obfuscates, or just skates, the audience will remain skeptical, verging on cynical. And every business leader sinks a little along with the speaker.

Respecting the Audience

Finally, it's about respecting your audience. Not settling for good enough but aspiring to deliver real value—ideas they can learn from, what-ifs that can stimulate new avenues of exploration, fresh opportunities, more informed public dialogue.

To get at that value, to build the brand—of the person and the organization—the speaker must connect with the audience in ways that most people just aren't doing today.

It's not hard. You just have to want to do it. And the more you invest, the greater the chance of significant return.

Key Points
Delivering memorable speeches builds your personal brand.

- A speech invitation is an opportunity; not an obligation.

- Demonstrable communications skills enhance your promotability.

- On the platform, mediocrity is never acceptable.

Notes

1. Peter Drucker, *The Essential Drucker* (New York: HarperBusiness, 2001).

2. Al Ries and Laura Ries, *The Fall of Advertising & the Rise of PR* (New York: HarperCollins, 2002).

3. Ibid, p. 91.

Tried . . . but Not Necessarily True

Snuck off to a matinee movie the other day, one of the great guilty pleasures of life. It's one thing to do a matinee on a weekend, for it's a sweet feeling to emerge from a cinema to see the sun still shining. But it's quite another to relax in front of a giant silver screen in a darkened theater when you know most of the rest of your world is staring at 15-inch computer monitors in 8-by-10-inch cubicles.

One thing did tarnish the moment, though—the trailers. These are invariably produced with great care and awesome effects. But too often, they're better than the movie, most of the time because they tell the whole story in 90 seconds, complete with the best explosions or funny bits. How many times have you seen a movie soon after having caught the preview, either in the theater or *ad nauseam* on television, and been disappointed because you felt like you'd just spent 15 bucks and two hours for *déjà vu* all over again? But no doubt you're wondering what this has to do with making a speech. A lot, I promise you.

For one thing, think about how your PowerPoint presentation will look to an audience that cut its media teeth on Titanic ship disasters and formidable matrixes. And who has $200 million to spend on effects for a speech, no matter how prestigious the audience?

For another thing, think about when it is that you start to lose interest in a novel or a movie. For me—and I'm not unusual, at least not in that way—it's when I can figure out the ending. Call me boring, but a car chase is a car chase. What matters is the resolution to the problem, the puzzle or the mystery set up in the early plot. If that resolution comes too soon, I'm outta there, at least in my head.

So why does every speechifying how-to book I've ever read continue to insist on the old tried-and-true model of speechmaking as the preferred blueprint? You probably know it:

Step 1: Tell 'em what you're gonna tell 'em

Step 2: Tell 'em.

Step 3: Tell 'em what you told 'em.

Step 4: Sit down and bask in the applause.

Please help me with this model. Do we really think the audience is so stupid that they need to hear the stuff three times? Do we need to treat our colleagues like recalcitrant school kids who can't follow a reasoned line of logic—or better, a story—without first telegraphing our message, then continually looping back to make sure they're still with us?

Please.

The old model is wrong. To put it more charitably, we've outgrown the old model because of the skills we've had to learn in a world where we have access to more information in a 24-hour period than the average person 500 years ago would come across in a lifetime.

Twenty years ago, teachers in training were advised that at any given time in any given class, about 10 percent of the students would be mentally elsewhere. The 10-percent-nonattention zone would migrate around the classroom, but only rarely would you have 100 percent of the class actually with the teacher—and that only when the teacher would throw chalk at some sleepyhead in the back row.

This, of course, was at the dawn of the MTV age. Now a whole generation has been weaned on visual and aural stimuli that change rapidly. Even in those early days, a three-minute-long music video would have 60–90 edits in it: i.e., the average shots lasted two to three seconds and many were not even that long. Talk about short attention span. Does the prefix "nano" come to mind?

Getting Their Attention . . . and Keeping It

Digital television, the Internet, e-mail, instant messaging—all these have only added to the expectation of instant gratification. Not interested in this video? Click. Here's another channel. Still not interested? Click. Let's hit ICQ and see who I can talk to.

In too much of a hurry to actually type full words? Let's invent shorthand codes to get the message across right away—and forget about upper and lower case. Then let's build the new pictographic language into the software. On my new computer, I try to type a colon followed by a right bracket, the "old" way to type the emoticon for a smile, to indicate a joke. What do I get? ☺. Yikes! In some ways it makes me ☹.

But in other ways it creates a real challenge for an old art form like the public speech. Because the people who live in this hyperpaced cyberworld are our audience. How can we possibly expect them to pay attention to someone talking for 20 minutes, especially when we tell 'em what we're going to tell 'em in the first two minutes, then spend 16 minutes telling 'em and the last two minutes making sure they heard what we told 'em?

And if they don't pay attention, they won't remember anything. Not you as the speaker. Not your company as a fascinating organization to work for or do business with. Not your content as the most insightful analysis of the market since Henry Ford figured out that Everyman wants affordable mobility.

And if they don't remember, why do it? Why invest the time or money to get the speech written, the slides prepared, for the coaching, the travel to get to the venue, and the personal investment of hours that could have been spent on something more productive?

It's really not enough to respond, "Because everyone else is doing it, and they expect me to do it too." Like your mother said, if everyone jumped off a cliff . . .

The good news is that if the old model is ready for a dignified retirement, if not burial, there are alternative strategies that work, strategies that don't insult the intelligence of the audience. They work because they are closely attuned to the fundamental ways in which human beings assimilate information and, just as important, seek their entertainment.

Ultimately, they work because they start where they should: with the audience, your key partner in this endeavor.

For make no mistake: First and foremost, a speech is a form of entertainment—pure live theater. And once you put bums in the seats, it's up to you to grab and keep their attention.

If you understand that, you are halfway there.

Start with the Audience

The scene's a familiar one in the executive office suites of our world. The PR official leads the consultant into an office already filled with suits.

"Joe, guys," she says, "this is W.R.D. Smith, the guy who's going to write the speech after we give him the content. W., this is Joe Bloggs, our CEO, Dan Pointer, the SVP of IT, Al Sterling, the CFO, and Bill Board, our Chief Marketing Officer."

There are handshakes all around, and then Bloggs gets down to business: "All right, folks, we've got to give the keynote at the WIPSAU conference next month. What are we gonna say?"

"Well, we gotta get that productivity message out there."

"Yeah, I've got a pretty solid slide deck on that."

"What about the streamlining? We've made good progress, and we can show how much we care, for employees and the shareholder!"

"Let's talk about our Q3 numbers—they're looking real good compared to Sinister Inc."

The suggestions flow, the writer scribbles notes. Bloggs listens, throws in a couple of ideas himself, then checks his watch. Running late again. "Ok, here's the deal," he says, restoring order to the meeting. "I want each of you guys to give me the top 20 slides you've created in the last, say, month, and send them to Pamela here, and she'll get them to the writer. Then, W., you can edit them down for us. And once we get the slides done, then you can write the notes around that."

It's a scene that repeats itself over and over in the corridors of corporate power. The details may change from place to place. Often the wordsmith is not even allowed at the table, corralled at a distance to interpret the speaker's wishes through the filter of the gatekeepers. But the generic response to a speech request is pretty standard. "We have to do this, so what are we going to say? what message do we have to get across?"

Trouble is, this is a cart-before-the-horse approach to a speech.

It reminds me of the time I was talking to a PR person for a major international manufacturing company where the media relations folks used to boast about the quantity of news releases they sent out. A day without a news release, they said, was like a day without sunshine—a waste.

I was impressed by this industriousness because I'd spent a lot of time in an organization that sent out maybe one or two releases a quarter. Then I asked how successful the news releases were. What was the pick-up rate by the media? The answer: Oh, we don't really track that. Then how do you know how successful your news release program is? Because we send out at least one a day. But what if no one reads them? Silence, not unlike the sound a tree makes when it topples in the forest and there is no one there to hear.

Inputs vs. Outcomes

They were totally focused on inputs, choosing to ignore outcomes. Not unusual, especially in public relations, where outcomes are notoriously difficult to measure and track. But that doesn't make it right.

In the same way, the first response most people have to the prospect of giving a speech is to focus on the input: What are we going to say? It may seem logical, but seeming is not being. By focusing first on what you're going to say, you effectively ignore what you want to get out of it. Not to mention giving short shrift to the most important part of the speechmaking equation—the audience.

Any communication requires at least three elements: one, some data to be communicated, even if only inferentially; two, a sender; and three, a receiver. Without all three you don't have a communication.

Unfortunately, the common approach looks only at the first two elements. This input focus considers the event predominantly from the point of view of the sender—the person speaking—and the stuff being pitched. Whether there's anyone there to catch is almost irrelevant.

Granted, at some time early in the process, someone will want a rundown on the makeup of the audience. Most often, the answer provided by the organizers or a PR person will be general in nature. Not uncommonly, it will be filtered to the speaker's ego. "Oh, you know, Mr. Bloggs, maybe some managers but mostly directors and VPs, even a few COOs."

Expect a few harrumphs about the usual suspects, and then it's back to figuring out how many slides are needed to fill the 30-minute slot. Back to the inputs.

But that kind of analysis—and I use the word generously—downplays the role of the most critical player in this event. The audience is the whole point of making the speech in the first place. Building the brand, selling the company, the cause and yourself.

Wouldn't it make more sense to begin at the end and work back? Begin with what you want the audience to do, or believe, at the end of the speech. Begin with the desired outcome and then figure out how to get there. What data do you need? What illustrations, if any? What linear logic . . . what leaps of faith?

So the first question to ask is this: What do I want this audience to do when I finish talking—beyond the standing ovation, that is? Only when you know that can you hope to build a speech that the audience will remember, that will build your brand.

The Golden Goals

In any speech there are only two outcomes you need:

1. The audience remembers YOU (in a positive way, of course).

2. The audience remembers your HEADLINE (also in a positive way).

Accomplish these golden goals, and you have extracted real value from the opportunity.

No doubt these goals seem modest in the extreme. But consider a couple of points.

First, remember the reality in which you're speaking. At a conference, you'll be just one of dozens of people this audience will listen to, if not hear. Even if you're the lone lunchtime speaker at a prestigious speakers' club, most of the people in attendance will be back at their desks, fully engaged in their real lives, within minutes of you saying "In conclusion . . ." and "Thank you." If you can be remembered despite that competition, you have won.

Second, never overestimate the ability of the modern human being to have information flow virtually uninterrupted in one ear and out the other without touching so much as one cell of gray matter.

I have been guilty of this optimism myself. At one company I worked for, we gathered the senior executives every January to speak to all-employee meetings. It was really more of a show than a meeting, with the executives talking for 10 or 15 minutes each, interspersed with videos and skits and other fun "motivational" stuff. We were big on interactivity, with employee MCs wandering into the audience from time to time to schmooze and generally provide comic relief. In substance, these kickoffs were supposed to review the results of the previous year and inform every employee of the priorities for the coming year.

This particular year, the leaders had settled on ten imperatives for the company to address, things like reducing customer churn, extending the reach of the communications network at the heart of the operation, controlling travel spending so we had more to invest in product innovation . . . that sort of thing.

About two-thirds of the way through the session, we had the CEO give his spiel, which consisted of listing the ten imperatives verbally, backed up with impactful (we thought) and very expensive (we knew) graphics on giant screens behind him. Ten minutes later, we brought all ten senior people out onto the stage, each with a sign with a word or two on it reiterating the priorities. Ten minutes after that, the MC went into the audience and asked people at random to name the ten imperatives.

None of the first five people she talked to could name even one. The next couple of people could name one or two each, but in five such meetings we never got more than half the imperatives fed back to us. And these weren't casual observers. These were folks whose bonuses for the year would depend on the degree to which they succeeded in living up to those imperatives.

The audience gave us great feedback for the fun quotient of the event. But we'd spent all that time on the inputs, and we didn't get the outcome we wanted, and needed. So we had to spend even more money throughout the year to find other ways to communicate those priorities. Mission not accomplished.

I'm happy to report that we did learn our lesson, though. The next year, we faced a similar range of issues, but saw that, in the end, it amounted to a need to push profits up by 7 percent, in any way we could. Thus, at the next senior management conference, we rolled up all the imperatives into a single headline: "The 7 percent solution." We had created a memorable goal. And the audience was engaged.

Remember: You are the water, and the audience is the horse. They have been led to you by a variety of means, for any number of reasons. Now you must make them drink. You have to connect with them, be memorable to them.

Key Points

- The conventional speech structure is tired: Look for another way to be memorable.

- Focus on outcomes first, then tailor inputs to meet objectives.

- Heed the two Golden Goals of giving a speech. Make sure:
  - The audience remembers you.
  - The audience remembers your headline.

Understanding the Audience

People will clap, pretty much no matter what. The question is, can you get them to clap for more than ten seconds? Can you get them to stand up while they clap? Or at least think "Wow!"

When I came home with a 52 in physics on my eleventh-grade Christmas report card, I went to my father in desolation. "How can I be a doctor with a mark like that?" I asked him. "I just don't get physics."

He looked at me and said: "Dream no small dreams."

Okay, I thought, nice sentiment (I thought it was his original epigram) but how is it relevant? "Persevere. Don't give up just because a couple of months of work in a new subject doesn't give you the results you want. Don't abandon that dream."

I listened, and went back after Christmas determined to work at physics. And I did. Hours of homework. Extra tutoring from Mr. Sheldrake. Picking the brains of the physics club president. The result: I raised my mark to 62. And I'm a writer, not a doctor, today. But that's okay. The idea is still a good one. Dream no small dreams, even when it comes to giving a speech.

That's why my counsel is that, as you contemplate whether or not to give a speech, as you develop your thoughts on what you want to get out of the opportunity, imagine the best possible outcomes. Then do everything in your power to make them become real.

Start with what could or should happen in the room itself as you speak. I want the audience to go "Ahhh," two or three times. I want them to think to themselves, "Gee, I didn't know that," or "Gee, that's interesting," half a dozen times. At the end, I want them to think I'm a pretty clever, talented, witty, charismatic person. And a standing ovation wouldn't be bad either.

The fact is, whenever and however you make a speech, people will clap. For some, it will be a thank-god-that's-over sort of applause. For others, it's a "Not bad, what's next?" For still others, "Well, I'm glad it was you and not me." No matter what you do or say, whether the slides work or not, people will acknowledge your effort by puttin' their hands together while you are in the house.

The challenge is to get them to clap for more than the perfunctory ten seconds before they scoot their chairs back and rush the exits. Sometimes, there's nothing you can do. Too many things, like the clock, conspire against you. Oftentimes as well, the subject matter does not lend itself to the kind of emotional response that underlies a standing O. People do get choked up about the regulation of television broadcasting, I suppose, or the changing nature of corporate oversight under Sarbanes-Oxley. But generally not in large groups. So keep your expectations within some realm of possibility.

In my twenty-plus years' experience, speakers with whom I've worked have been given an SO just a handful of times. One was from an audience of teachers who had been singled out by a large corporation as part of an innovative program to promote schooling in science and engineering. Another was from a mixed audience of English Canadians responding to the CEO's impassioned plea for French Canadians to reject a plan to turn the province of Quebec into a separate country.

But there is a large realm of possibility beyond polite applause. And when you make the connection, when the speech works, when the dream comes true, you not only feel great, you also know you have added significantly to your personal brand and that of your cause.

So start small. Time the applause the next time you speak—or better, have someone do it for you (it looks a little bit less self-involved). Then set a target for the next time to lengthen the applause. If you get a couple of people standing up, then next time, make it six. It's just like managing financials—set objectives and then develop the tactics to hit the numbers. You're making the investment. You should make sure you get the most out of it. And like they say, what gets measured gets done.

The tactics you use are virtually unlimited. But always, always, they should be based on the fundamental need to connect with the audience.

An Audience Is Not a Mob

That's easier said than done, of course, for a couple of fundamental reasons that should be considered when you're focusing on the outcome.

Most important, an audience is not a mob. It doesn't think as one. Its members don't all perceive information the same way; they don't all process it the same way; they certainly don't all respond and react the same way; and they all have a different relationship with you, the speaker, from intimate to none at all.

People are different. At some level, we all know this. And have known it for some time. As early as 1836, the physician Marc Dax noticed that of the 40 of his patients who had lost the ability to speak, every one of them had sustained damage to the left brain.

It took another 70 years before anyone noticed that people with right brain damage tended to have spatial troubles. But today it's common knowledge that the two hemispheres of the brain tend to do different and separate jobs. The left brain tends to be more rational, responsible for mathematics and verbal skills. Our education system, including IQ tests, and our reward system in the business world tend to reward left brain skills—dispassionate logic. So too when people are consuming goods and making decisions on the rational basis of price—the left brain is in charge.

However, there is ample evidence that the right side of the brain is the home of long-term memory, emotion, and, importantly, meaning. This is where the rules of syntax, or mathematics, are massaged by the perception of context, of a bigger structure. For example, the composer Ravel was stricken by a stroke in the left side of his brain, leaving him unable to read, write, or play music. But he could tell if a piano was out of tune, or if a musician made a mistake in a concert because his right brain could still "see" the pattern, even if it could not articulate the rules.

In any given audience you will have some proportion that is influenced more by its left brain (these folks tend to be the engineers, scientists, and accountants of the world) and some part that is the touchy-feely right-brain crowd (the so-called creative and caring functions, HR, marketing, etc.).

Complicating that scenario is the fact that, even among outwardly rational people, brand choices are often the result of preferences based in the emotional centers of the right brain. Once I chose to buy a Honda for whatever emotional reasons (wanting to be seen as environmentally conscious, or a pioneer or whatever), my left brain then kicked in to provide the justification (or rationalization, depending on your point of view).

Now it's true that certain brain dominance types tend to gather in certain functions. If you're facing an audience of accountants or computer geeks, you can safely posit they've get a lot of left-brain power engaged. But even in relatively homogenous groups there is still a continuum of variation among individuals, driven by sharp differences in professional opinion, preferences, jealousies, and even politics, all of which color the way in which your inputs are perceived and received. If you've ever been privy to a debate between academics, you understand a little about the gulf that often divides even like-minded people

Not only that, but the left-right brain dichotomy doesn't begin to capture the complexity of the audience—or the challenge you have to be memorable for at least a majority of the people who show up.

Simply put, different people learn differently. And learning is a pretty good proxy for being memorable. One could spend a useful lifetime examining the literature on how people learn. But we don't have a lifetime. We've got a speech to write and deliver. So let's cut to the good bits.

In your audience you will not only have right- and left-brain-dominant folks, you will also have people with different learning styles. Some are stimulated by visual stimuli above all else. Some by auditory cues. Some learn best only by doing. How do you make a connection with all those types? How do you become memorable? You're not a three-ring circus.

Memory Fails Us

You also face the challenge of our time: We live in an age when memory matters only in computers—or so it seems. In fact, much of today's entertainment industry apparently relies on the fact that we have let our collective memory get flabby as it serves up warmed-over rehashes of dead sitcoms and old thrillers masqu-erading as computer-enhanced theatrical blockbusters. But that's another issue.

What is more relevant to us, as we try to be memorable from a speaking platform, is that as our society creates more artificial memory in our machines, we have indeed become indifferent to the innate store-and-forward capabilities of our own brains. Memory is simply not as important to us as it was to our ances-tors.

This is not just an Information Age phenomenon. In fact, there is an argument to be made that the decline of human memory began with Gutenberg and his moveable type. Once everyone, more or less, had access to the very efficient knowledge storage technology known as books, people didn't have to remember nearly so much. They could just look it up. Ask Casey Stengel.

Of course, our times have accelerated the withering of our memory as more and more of humanity's hard-won knowledge is easily and swiftly accessible through the plethora of new tech-nologies.

My children never knew the chore—nor the beauty—of mem-ory work in school. What a loss this is, to consign such a power-ful, evocative skill to electronic warehouses. No wonder our jaws drop in awe when we contemplate the ancient orators and poets who could recite hours-long epics, verbatim, from memory. It is said that Seneca the Elder, who lived at the time of Christ, would wow his students by asking each person in a class of 200 pupils to make up one line that, once all had spoken, would form a long poem. After the last student had spoken, Seneca would then re-cite each line back, in reverse order.

How many of us today could do one-tenth of that? How many of us live in fear that our lives will be destroyed if we lose our PalmPilots with their records of our phone numbers and, holy of holies, passwords? Memory fails, but not the electronic minder, at least as long as you replace the battery. But the device even reminds you to do that.

Before books, memory was everything.

If you gave a speech in those days—which was the golden age of rhetoric for many people—you'd face an audience that was accustomed to using their brains to remember things. Even those not schooled at the feet of Socrates had to commit to memory the ins and outs of their craft and the ups and downs of their personal histories.

Today, we are bombarded with thousands of messages every day—e-mail, voice mail, snail mail, telephone calls, advertisements, Internet spam. In fact, every three years, the amount of information we need to run our lives doubles.[1] So our key survival skill is not so much being able to remember stuff but rather being able to forget stuff. We have programmed ourselves to tune out very quickly, to filter that which does not have immediate, tangible relevance.

It has to be that way or we'd never get through our day. But it sure makes it tough if your goal is to cut through all that white noise and not only be heard but also be remembered.

You have to connect with your audience at some level deeper than an opening joke. And because of the speed with which your audience reacts in this MTV world, you have to do it fast.

So what do you do? I've sometimes toyed with the idea of piping a wonderful aroma into the air of a meeting room because everyone knows that catching a whiff of a favorite scent can instantly evoke strong memories and warm feelings. Plus, that's one trick I haven't ever seen done yet, so you've got the elements of surprise and innovation.

It might work, but it can be risky, because one person's cinnamon toast may be another's swamp gas. (Women, for instance, don't respond nearly as strongly to pumpkin pie as men.) And it's also tough to find an odor that evokes record profits, since I have yet to hear of anyone bottling the smell of money.

That said, though the tactic may be a bit off the wall, the strategy is sound because it addresses how memories are made.

Meaning and Memory

The human brain has about 10 billion neurons or nerve cells. They are connected by an immensely complex network of dendrites, something on the order of 1,000 trillion connections. So the possible number of different connections inside our heads is about $10^{1,000,000}$. Ouch.

Being a right-brainer, I can't even visualize such a number. It is meaningless to me so I know I'll never remember it. However, what gives these data some meaning for me is the simple observation that all these connections represent a storage and retrieval system for data that we call memory. The stronger the memory, the easier it is for us to make the right connections from where our thought starts to where the memory resides.

Like the Internet, the path to any given memory can take any number of different routes. But a strong memory is like a Web cookie—the path is well worn and easy to travel.

What clears that path is not, it turns out, rote memory work, like memorizing a Frost poem and being able to regurgitate the states and their capitals. Rather, it is the way the individual constructs his or her own meaning around the memory. Meaning that derives from a sense of the whole created by all the bits of data taken together. The forest rather than just the trees.

Ask any actor. They don't memorize lines. They *learn* them, applying their own often idiosyncratic tricks to put the script within a context that holds meaning for them. "What's my motivation?" has become a trite joke about struggling thespians. But it's really a fundamental question they ask to put some meaning around the cold, hard, unpatterned words on the pages of the script.

Fundamentally, the meanings on which memory is based are a function of our ability to recognize or create patterns. Our brains are like giant microprocessors, operating both at the detailed level and at the more holistic level, and doing it simultaneously. And while bits of data may dazzle us like a gold nugget in the river bed, what makes them memorable is the bigger picture—where there's one nugget, there must be more.

Patterning—the creation of meaning and memorability—all that is centered in the right side of the brain, close to the emotional core of any individual's being.

Oh, the humanity!

Shared Experiences

So, you're faced with the objective of being memorable to this crazy quilt of individuals in front of you, all of whom perceive and react to the world in different ways. Left brain, right brain, visual learners, auditory learners, tactile learners, thinker/observers, feeler/doers, and on and on.

What do you do?

You send in your go-to guy: your humanity. It is the one and only thing you have that connects you with every single person in every single audience.

You take the shared experience of what it means to be a functioning human being in the twenty-first century and drive it into the right brains of every person there—even the left-brainers. You can follow it up with as much logical, rational discussion as you want—as long as you start and end in the right brain, with the meaning, with the memorability.

Everyone has shared experiences. All of us have despaired at the long line of brake lights ahead of us during rush hour. All of us have curiosity. We all stand in awe in the presence of great courage or prodigious talent.

Somewhere deep inside even the most virtuous of us, there's a little place that glories in the failures of others—I've often thought the Darwin awards provide a rich vein of material for audience connectivity.

All of us have fears—spiders, snakes, heights, clowns. "What? Admit I have a phobia? You must be crazy. I'm a Captain of Industry!!!" Relax there, *mon capitaine*. Vulnerability does not show weakness; it shows humanity; it builds credibility. It makes you memorable and builds your brand.

There's a wonderful old saying in live theater: "Heart line, then plot line." It's good advice whenever you're in front of an audience, whenever you want to be remembered.

Key Points

- Audience members learn and perceive differently.

- Meaning and context build memories.

- Share your humanity first.

Note

1. From a presentation to Bell Canada by Bill Jensen, CEO, The Jensen Group, Morristown, N.J., August 17, 2003.

Performance Ready

The house lights dim. The rustling stills. The whispers stop.

A spotlight picks out a solitary figure on stage, facing into the darkness that envelopes an audience full of eager faces, open minds. Anticipation builds as the hush deepens. The person on stage fiddles with a prop, takes a breath.

"Madame chairman, colleagues, friends."

The spell is shattered . . .

"Thank you for that kind introduction. It is my pleasure to be here today. The topic of your conference reminds me of that old story of the three fishermen in the rowboat . . ." What started with all the promise of a Broadway blockbuster has ended, in a matter of seconds, with the conventional whimper, one more forgettable wavelet in a Sargasso Sea of sluggish syntax.

Who among us has not seen this happen? Okay, maybe not the spotlight—although it's common enough for corporate shows. But all the rest of it, almost every time you see a speech or a presentation. *Why* does this happen, and happen repeatedly? Safety in numbers? Laziness? Lack of nerve (to put it politely)? Maybe a bit of each? But maybe it's simple ignorance, and I use that word in the least judgmental way possible, the way one would describe an inhabitant of the Gobi desert who is, by dint of his location and priorities, ignorant of the tortured love life of J.Lo.

Hard Data Do Not a Speech Make

Far too many people—speakers and their support teams included—just don't know what a speech can and cannot achieve. They're ignorant of the limits and the strengths of the medium. They see the speech as a chance to transmit reams of information about their cause. Sometimes it's a baffle-'em-with bullshit strategy. But most often it's a genuine attempt to provide the audience with plenty of hard data to prove that Acme Widgets is indeed the manufacturer of choice, with world-class quality and customer care skills up to here.

"Numbers," the speaker says. "Give me lots of numbers. People like numbers because they're real."

Maybe. But Mark Twain, the man who equated statistics with damn lies, might differ. Whether numbers are real or not, I am not the person to say. (I dropped math when my high school teachers began talking about imaginary roots in calculus.) And I know that some people do like numbers, love them, in fact. But to build a speech on them is to break out the Sominex. Same with lists and lists of facts. Pass the NoDoz.

Consider this. The average person reads to himself at about 250 words a minute. Assuming that, like the kids at Lake Wobegon, all the members of a typical audience for your speech are above average, that means a whole bunch of people can read pretty fast, up to 400 or 500 words a minute.

On the other hand, the average person talks—or reads out loud—at about 100 to 150 words a minute. Too much faster, and one gets tongue-tied.

So if I want information about something—cold hard facts—the most efficient way to get them is to read about them. If I want data on a company, I'll look at the annual report—or go online to see what's new and who's who and what the media are saying.

In about 20 minutes or so, I can amass a huge amount of information and learn what I need to know. And I don't have to leave my keyboard, or spend thousands of dollars to travel to hear the CEO tell me the same thing.

Reading is fundamentally a more efficient way to pick up raw *information* than having someone talk about it. That's one reason that instructional videos—particularly for corporate training—sit on shelves pretty much every day until they're obsolete. People can get the information they need in much less time by consulting a manual somewhere. And people are looking for every opportunity to save time in our fast-forward society. So why do they continue to look forward to attending speeches in person? Why don't they just ask for the text to be sent to them, or posted on a Web site? Well, they do that too. But they still attend in person, by the hundreds of thousands.

Why? Because a speech is less about information transfer and more about human-to-human stimulation. Just like theater. Why does live theater flourish even though special effects technicians can treat movie and television audiences to almost unimaginable spectacle anywhere in the known universe . . . and beyond? It's certainly not because of a cost-benefit analysis. Even at $15 a pop, a ticket to the movies is multiple times less expensive than a loge on Broadway.

Why does theater flourish when so often it's unreal? How often, after all, do people break into song and dance in the middle of life? It's because we retain some innate need to connect with other people *in person*, to marvel at talent in the raw, even if separated from it by footlights and the language of a playwright who has been dead for nearly 400 years.

That's the opportunity a speech represents: to connect on a human level, even if it's from the height of a podium. A speech—even a boardroom presentation—is live theater that enables the audience to get an extraordinary insight into and perspective on the speaker's intellect, character and the quality of the organization he represents. You're not likely to get up and start saying, "To be or not to be." But the connection you're going for is exactly the same. For the best speeches are extended soliloquies that lay out the core issues and in so doing reveal what kind of organization—and person—is grappling with them.

Granted, a speech is about the transmission of information. It's just not necessarily—or even primarily—information as the propeller heads and bean counters usually define it. It's not about quarterly results, or new products or even promises of new products—details that form what you might call the plumbing of the content. Rather, it's about the connections between the data points, the trends that are developing. It's about ideas, not facts, although facts are often more useful than not in supporting ideas. Above all, it's about the person delivering the goods, inspiring confidence in himself and his cause, driving the value of his personal brand.

The Speech as Drama

Most people, most of the time, will walk away from a memorable speech with only one or two key points stuck in their brains. Those points could be interesting statistics; they could be particularly impressive revenues, although in an afternoon in which a conference attendee can easily catch a dozen or more presentations, whether your revenue growth hit 33 percent or 37 percent is probably not going to stick in the mind. But more likely, the key memories will revolve around either a novel idea or a perception—positive or negative—of the person doing the talking. In fact, ideas—especially big ideas—are almost always more effectively conveyed in person because the audience perceives not only the lucidity of the argument but also the enthusiasm, expertise, and salesmanship of the proponent. To a large degree, the message is in the medium. Of course, the audience's perception of the speaker rests on a host of elements, from the cogency of the material to his or her physical attractiveness—like it or not, audiences do respond more and more positively to good-looking people with pleasant voices and strong, confident deliveries.

Most important, what makes a memorable speech is the same thing that makes a memorable stage play—the quality of the connection between the audience and the player. It's a connection that can be established in any number of ways—shared experience, an offbeat observation, humor—depending on the wants, needs, and abilities of both the audience and the speaker. But whatever method is used, the connection must be made, or you're wasting your time and that of the audience. And time remains our most critical nonrenewable resource.

OK, you ask, if a speech is a theatrical performance, what clues does that provide for making the connection with the audience? What tools does the playwright bring to the task? And the actors? How do they engage the audience and make an impression that lasts long after the last encore? Books have been written about the power of theater. But they all boil down to one thing: entertainment. It can be the flash and froth of a *42nd Street* or the life and death struggles of a redundant salesman. Theater engages our senses, our sensibilities. It makes us aware of the subtleties and ironies of life.

Audiences bring to the theater their willing suspension of disbelief, their ability to enter an often unreal world presented on stage. No one believes the dancing street gangs in *West Side Story* are real. But they're willing to extend their imagination to enjoy the sublime music and dance, to sympathize with the characters and their limited choices, to see their own lives in a hard-edged view of human nature.

Similarly, giving a speech is an activity far removed from reality. You are creating an event that is something very few of us do ever, let alone every day. When you stand up to make a speech, the audience is prepared to believe you can interest them just by talking for 20 minutes. In exchange, like a playwright and actor rolled into one, you provide enlightenment, entertainment.

In the theater, it happens in any number of ways: intricate plotting, interesting characters; conflict, suspense, surprise, wit . . . an appeal to the imagination . . . a challenge to safe, conventional thinking . . . smart stagecraft . . . romance . . . and on and on.

Most of those tools can be in your speaker's kit. Probably not romance, but other than that, they're all open to you. Your text is your script, your plot. Most speeches have no plot, and damn few surprises. As for suspense, well, that goes out the door as soon as the speaker says, "These are the areas I will cover today." The audience may not literally head for the exits, but that kind of clumsy forewarning tends to encourage people to check out before the third act. It takes forethought to build in some drama, some entertainment into the structure of your speech.

As for characters, well, there are two: you and the audience. Those strangers in the room are active participants in your speech. Their part is to engage in the virtual dialogue with open and active minds. You will probably not hear the wheels spinning in their heads as you speak, but you will be able to see it in their attentive eyes. You drive the plot; they respond. If you're doing it right, they will be telling you through their body language that they are fully engaged in the journey with you.

As for you, well, clearly you are playing a lead role. Your costume sets the scene. Your words can unleash the imaginative power of the listeners. You can touch them as a human being first, then use that connection to cement your case.

You needn't be—you probably can't be—Hamlet. And you certainly don't have the Bard of Stratford writing for you. But you can, in your words and in your demeanor, understand that when you've giving a speech, you are giving a theatrical performance. You must entertain and challenge, you must bring imagination and creativity, even as you strive to inform, persuade, and teach.

Part III of this book gives you some creative ways to create your persona and capture the interest of your audience. Part IV helps you write the script, and Part V assists with tips on delivery.

But first, let's consider whether you should even take the role as in Part II we look at essential questions to ask before you agree to take the stage.

Key Points

- A speech is not about facts and numbers; it's about story, meaning.

- A speech is live theater.

- A memorable speech rests on the quality of the connection between the speaker and the audience.

- Use techniques of theater—plot, character, suspense—to connect.

Before Saying Yes

Talk is cheap because supply exceeds demand.

—Anonymous

5

You're the Star

Remember when you were ten years old? At recess, your secret crush pulled you aside and handed you a small square envelope. You ripped it open: a clown-faced invitation. A birthday party. Balloons. Presents! Cake!! Ice cream!!! Spin the bottle!!!??!! You wouldn't dream of saying no. Even if your tonsils were on fire. There simply was no option. You'd been *chosen*.

Today, you're, well, older than ten. The invitation comes in the mail—snail or e-, it doesn't matter.

"As the Chairperson of the events committee of the Wall Drug Chamber of Commerce, it is my great pleasure to invite you to be the keynote speaker at our Annual General Meeting. As you are a renowned expert in your field and a compelling speaker, we feel confident that you will give our members tremendous insight into the keys to success in business as you see them. While we cannot pay you for your appearance, we can reimburse you for all reasonable expenses while in Wall Drug, the bumper sticker capital of the Southeast. I will be contacting you in person shortly to . . ."

Well, not quite as exciting as a birthday party at your crush's house. But you've always been intrigued by those roadside signs and bumper stickers exhorting you to visit Wall Drug. And hey, they seem to know you—"renowned expert"?—Yup, got that right. "Compelling speaker"? Uh-huh.

Why not? Because flattery is a trick known to the oldest professionals in the book. And when you hear it, the red flags had better go up, if not the red lights. Because the fact is that there are some hard questions to ask well before agreeing to speak anywhere. They are questions that may test your ego, especially if it's been well buttered up by the compliments of the hosts. But they will serve to build your credibility, manage your brand, and enable you to be memorable—at a place and time of your choosing.

For that is the issue in the end. As much as you have to understand and play to the interests of the audience, it's all about that most fundamental of human questions: What's in it for me?

The Power Is Yours

People who ask you to do things for them have an agenda. Usually, big surprise, your goals, preferences, wants, and desires are not at the top of it. That's the first thing to remember when you're invited to speak at a conference or a luncheon. There may be genuine interest in what you have to say and who you are. But above and beyond all that, the organizers' objective is to stage a great event. You are a means to *their* end.

Their end may be to fill the seats of their conference on the promise of a panel discussion dust-up between and among the heavyweights in the field. And you'll hear words like "great opportunity to set the record straight" or "confront the issues" or "engage in a frank, substantive dialogue" to encourage your participation.

But what do you gain by sharing the spotlight with a contender? Maybe something. Maybe nothing, or worse.

Their end may be just to get a big name to talk about the all-embracing "topic of your choice." In these cases, you can almost taste the treacle in their words: "You're such a leader, your presence is such a compelling one, our members would love to hear your views on virtually anything you want to talk about." Your teeth should be hurting by now. All manner of ego-expanding thoughts can enter your mind at a time like this, from Sally Field's "They really like me" to "I can show that so-and-so who's better." Oh yes, the testosterone does start pumping, even in the women.

But these thoughts obscure the key, fundamental power relationship that's going on here, a relationship you must keep in mind as you make your decisions about when and where to speak. And it is this: The people who extend the invitation need you more than you need them. You are in the driver's seat.

That is true from the moment you receive the invitation until you step down from the podium. It is true as you plan what to speak about, how long you will speak, what props or support you will use, the setup of the dais. You are the one who has to be comfortable, with everything around this appearance. The burden of supplying that comfort rests on them. You are the person with the knowledge, the title, the reputation, the whatever. You are the person the audience is expected to respond to, to remember. It is your reputation that is on the line.

Yes, the organizers need to protect their brand, but that is not your problem. You, personally, are the one on stage. You, personally, are the one whose words will live, or not, after the event. You are the talent without which the organizers don't have much of a show. And that's why you have the upper hand.

Exercise Your Control

You still have to work to please the audience, because ultimately they have the power to decide if your appearance was successful or not. But you have the clout when it comes to every element of how you're going to please them. The best events will be when your interests and those of the organizers—and the audience—come together. Synchronicity, they call it, and it's a very good thing. But it cannot be serendipitous. It cannot be left to chance.

Every element is important. Worry about every single one of them. And exercise your power. Case in point: I once found myself in discussion with a CEO who had been invited to make a dinner speech at an important venue. He wanted to do the event, but something was sticking in his craw. And it didn't take too large a crowbar to get it out.

"Cocktails at 6:30. Dinner—with wine—at 7:30. Then I get up at 8:30 to try to dazzle an audience that is full and slightly drunk (if not more). And all of us have probably been up since 6 in the morning, not to mention jet lag, etc., etc. I talk for half an hour, and then everybody's looking at their watches and hurrying out to get home so they can at least get six hours' sleep before it starts again. No wonder people don't ever remember what I say."

We commiserated together awhile until he had one of those moments of blindingly simple insight: What would they say if I told them I want to speak *before* the dinner, he said. Bingo.

We considered scheduling the speech even before the cocktails, but shelved that as both impractical and not optimal. After all, while we didn't want the audience dozy with drink, it was okay if they'd had a belt or two to soften them up, make them more receptive. So we put together a couple of arguments for moving the talk to a spot after the national anthem but before grace for the meal. Apart from the obvious, we reasoned, there's also the added benefit that if you give your speech before the meal, the audience then has the chance to hash it over as they eat. It helps them get over those awkward silences when the small talk runs out, and makes what you've said more memorable because it's repeated and maybe even debated while the audience breaks bread. Plus, if people have to leave early, for instance to head back to the office if it's a luncheon speech, they leave the meal, not the feast of ideas you're presenting.

Well, the organizers bought the argument, and from that time on, speaking before the meal became the standard operating procedure for this executive. Clearly, it's not an idea that has caught on with most event organizers, for I still attend session after session where I struggle through small talk during the meal, then listen to the speech and rush out the door with the rest of the stampede as the master of ceremonies wraps it up. But perhaps that is not surprising in a field where traditions and conventions seem frozen in another time, and change arrives with glacial speed.

Act Like a Major Leaguer

All this talk about the speaker's being in the driver's seat is fair enough, I can hear you think. But what if I'm just starting out and I need some appearances to build my reputation? I don't have much power. What if I'm willing to play the sticks, as it were, to pay my dues in Podunkville, to take whatever the organizers will give me?

Well, in communications—as in life—there are damn few absolutes. We do need to compromise. We do need, on occasion, to take one for the team by heading out into a blizzard to speak to the local Knights of Columbus when the boss tells us to. We are going to be stuck into the 4:30 p.m. time slot on the last day of the conference, just before the cocktail hour for the celebratory gala. The fact is that a few character-builders won't hurt. They'll help you find out what works and what doesn't in terms of meeting the expectations of the audience. They'll build the necessary scars that will protect you in virtually any situation. The trick is to minimize the number of times you're boxed in with few choices. And even when you're stuck, assert yourself.

For that's the critical point: You can't learn to do things right if you accept doing things wrong. If you get into the habit of letting the events chairman of the local Chamber dictate your topic, the time you're going to speak, the kind of microphone, whatever, you may never learn, you may never exercise your right to make a name for yourself and your cause your way.

When the Baltimore Orioles were the winningest team in baseball through the 1960s and 1970s (you could look it up), they practiced something call The Oriole Way. All their players did certain fundamental things the same way. And when I say all their players, I mean *all* their players, from Brooks and Frank Robinson at Memorial Stadium right down to the rawest recruit in the scrubeenie minors. Now 90 percent–plus of these Rookie League players would never even get a whiff of a cup of coffee in The Show. But their managers, coaches, and mentors were insistent: Do things the major league way.

When I was freelance talent scout for the fledgling Kansas City Royals, I received a whole package of charts and instructions on how to record the relative merits of the sandlot hopefuls I followed around. After a couple of weeks, I thought I'd found two or three new phenoms, kids who were head and shoulders above their peers.

But when I called my kindly old mentor in Rochester, he asked me a few pointed questions.

"How fast does Pfaff make it from home to first on a ground ball?"

I gave him a number.

"Well, Willie Wilson does it half a second faster."

But Pfaff's just a kid and he's the best on his team, probably in the league.

"But he's not close to major league standard, and he's only a couple of years younger than Wilson. You've got to judge these kids on how they might do as a big leaguer, not how they do against their current competition. Keep looking."

It was the second hard lesson baseball had taught me. (The first was when this same old kindly mentor, himself a full-time scout, assessed me after a tryout camp in which I was clearly one of the superior players: "Good hands, great attitude, no wheels. Stay in school." So much for that dream.)

If you want to be a major leaguer, act like one. If you want to be the next Winston Churchill or Bill Clinton (as an orator, I mean), act like them. Treat every opportunity as an important building block. Expect the best, and you'll be surprised how often you get it.

Take a cue from Broadway. Try things out in low-risk, local opportunities. Take your pitch on the road to hone it for the day you play the Great White Way. But always, always be true to your objectives. And insist on your due as the star of the show.

In that context, there are some critical questions you must ask yourself before you succumb to the flattery of the invitation and set the production in motion. The following chapter sets out the most critical to consider.

Key Points

- Be aware of the agenda of those who invite you to speak.

- You have the power—exercise it.

- Success is in the details.

- To be major league, act major league.

Do I Really Need to Do This?

Always, always, the first question to ask when you're invited to speak is, what's your objective? What would you want to get out of it?

The second is just as important: given your objective, is this an audience you need to reach?

Most times during the day, when I say something, no one applauds. And I'm not alone. So when you get an invitation, it can be nice to fantasize that there may be an opportunity to hear that approval in a very tangible way and not worry too much about the source. But given what it costs in time, effort, and real dollars to put on a first-rate presentation, there is a clear business imperative to worry about just that.

Would you go to Florida to set up your downhill ski store? Of course not. There are no hills. What's more, your ideas, even your very presence, is your currency as you build your personal brand and that of your cause. You don't want to spend it in the wrong places. Nor do you want to devalue it by popping up at every event going, like some sort of manic huckster.

So you have to carefully consider how important the audience is to you. Are they customers? Prospects? What's the predominant job title—is this a group of first-level managers or are they

VPs and above? What's the predominant professional affiliation? Are these technical people or wacky marketing types?

Will there be a significant contingent of influencers, people who know people who can amplify your insights across complex networks of discussion, even gossip? What about media? Will they be there to provide their own powerful spin to your words?

The answers to these questions will not give you a simple go-no-go decision on being part of the show. That will change depending on your objectives. What exactly is it you see coming out of this appearance? For example, you may want major exposure for an initiative. You may want to send up a trial balloon for some policy proposal. You may want to simply help educate people about your cause and why it should be important to them. You may want to position yourself as a thought leader, not necessarily direct-selling your organization, but soft-selling it through the reflected glow of your well-considered opinions on public policy issues.

Whatever your objective is, having a clear one will help determine whether you should accept the invitation.

Also, you may want to try things out with an audience of first-level managers. But if your objective is to influence policy, that sort of audience is not likely to be your choice. You may want to speak peer-to-peer to VPs and above (or knock their socks off if you're a lowly manager). It is quite possible, even likely, that you will be making speeches where you want no media coverage. If that's your objective, it's an easy call to turn down an invitation to an event that includes the media.

Fundamentally, you have to ask questions that will assure you that there is some significant overlap between your objectives and the interests of the audience. It's not something Broadway stars have to do. They can pretty well count on having most of their audience predisposed to the suspension of disbelief that lies at the core of any great theatrical experience. But for a speaker? Not so much. You're faced with people who take in information in a wide variety of ways, people who have different reasons for being there, many of which may not include you or your cause or anything you might say.

So ask questions up front. Let's say you're a big-picture marketing type who likes ideas at the 50,000-foot level. If you're invited to speak to an audience of mid-level IT, or finance, or quality control managers, you might want to think more than twice. These people, by training if not by nature, look at their world differently than you do yours. And although they may appreciate an elegant solution, they like to know how the plumbing works. They connect with details.

This is not to say unequivocally that this is not the audience for you. Rather it is just to highlight that if you choose to enter this den of detail, you had better adopt an approach that will go at least halfway to meeting their needs.

Check Your Ego

Just as important, you must ask yourself some questions the answers to which you may not like. Consider this: The invitation floats onto your desktop to speak on the Changing Competitive Nature of the Widget Market. Now, you know a little bit about this topic. After all, you're in the business. But your rival . . . er . . . colleague knows a heck of a lot more about it and could deliver this talk with great panache. Are you the best person for the opportunity? Depends who's asking, and what your agenda is. From the organization's point of view, clearly the subject matter expert is the person to call on, especially if this person is a presentable speaker. But from your own personal branding point of view, the issue is much less clear. You could probably do a creditable, if unmemorable, job. On the other hand, you could acquire some brownie points for use at a later time by letting your colleague run with the assignment. He or she owes you, and your bosses, as long as they know the sacrifice you made, will know that you took one for the team.

As usual, there is no right or wrong answer to a question such as that. But that doesn't mean it shouldn't be asked. As a speaker, you're on a very public platform, not just for the audience in the room, but also for others in your circle who may be assessing your judgment, your character, and your willingness to be a team player. Whether you accept an invitation, reject it outright, or pass it along to someone whose expertise more closely matches the opportunity, any and all of those decisions and actions will be seen as part of who you are, the attributes of your brand.

Is This the Right Medium?

Once you figure that there will be enough people in the audience whom you want to reach, and you're the right person for the job, you still have to ask more fundamental questions.

Start with the medium itself. You want to communicate your message to these people, but is a speech the best way to do it? Remember that speeches have limitations. They are, by their nature, not good for the transmission of hordes of facts. That's true whether you're in the middle of a pack of speakers on a panel or you're all alone as the star of a gala luncheon.

Think about it. How many menus do you remember? If you're like me, none. Yet they're filled with facts, with language that evokes mouth-watering images of dishes even Wolfgang Puck would kill for. Yet the people who put menus together understand the role of the medium: It's to convey what's on offer, make it appealing in whatever way the clientele would define appealing, and then be put away when the real business—the consumption of food and drink—begins. Menus do not belong on the table once the salad appears. And menus of facts and figures and long lists of data, don't belong in speeches, because people simply will not remember them.

A speech is more about synthesis, about ideas and even emotion. Looking for trends in all the right places. Evoking the sense that the speaker is master of his or her domain, not because he or she can spout the revenue figures for the last 12 quarters, but because there is, in the analysis and commentary, some evidence of intelligence. Some sense that here is a person who knows what's going on.

So if your objective has more to do with providing the receivers of your message with reams of facts to sway their decision to support your organization, you may want to take a pass. You could turn your data into a white paper and distribute it with a personal note and a follow-up phone call. I just came from a liquor store where they were featuring giant ceramic hand-painted beer jugs, full of course, aimed for the gift-giving market. For what it costs you to create and give a speech, you could—if you were so inclined—send one of these to each of the 100 top people you want to reach with a CD coaster that contains all the relevant information. And you might get more people to pay attention. Less radically, it could be more effective to implement a broader public relations campaign, using the third-party endorsement of media coverage to legitimize your points.

On the other hand, if what you want to say has a strong emotional core, a compelling story, a solid connection with the humanity in all (or most) of us, then a speech is one of your best options. You and the audience—live, real-time, warts and all.

There is an instant credibility factor that few other vehicles can match, not even an appearance on *Oprah*.

You Want Me to Share the Spotlight?

From before kindergarten we are taught that sharing is good, selfishness is bad. Well, yes and no, at least when it comes to making speeches.

By far the majority of invitations you are likely to get will be to speak as part of a panel of experts at a conference. It only stands to reason. On a given day at a given conference there will be two or three keynote speeches and as many as a dozen panel sessions, each with three or four speakers plus a moderator who as often as not turns a simple Master of Ceremonies role into yet another opportunity to chime in with his or her detailed perspectives on the question at hand.

Organizers love a panel because it enables them to claim they have given the audience the broadest possible spectrum of expertise on a given topic in a very short time. It also lets them imply, suggest, hope for some sparks between and among people with different views. And no question, a good verbal sparring match can be a real audience pleaser.

But a panel might not work for you. Because you'll be one of several speakers, you'll have to be just that much more scintillating to break through the blizzard of words that is buffeting the audience. Of course, after having read this book, being scintillating won't be a problem. But there are other issues.

For one, how does appearing on a panel affect your personal brand, or that of your organization? There are many CEOs who refuse outright to appear on panels. "Keynote or nothing" is their point of view. And it is a valid one. Like any speaker, a CEO is his or her organization's brand incarnate at the moment of the speech, only more so. He or she also carries the weight of the highest and most powerful office in the organization. It's about star power, even in an age when boardroom scandals have tarnished the reputation of business executives in general.

So the question becomes, should a CEO share the spotlight? Most times, my answer would be no if the organization is a leader in its sector. Being the leader of one of these institutions should command a premium. It's not unlike the way car companies used to price their product. The margins on a Lincoln Continental were significantly larger than those on the Fairlane, Galaxy 500, or Pinto simply because of the cachet of the nameplate. People were willing to pay for the reputation as much as for the steel and leather and rubber. If your nameplate says CEO, that should command a premium. And in our context, that premium should be a single spotlight, trained on you and you alone.

Obviously there are judgments to be made based on cases. For instance, more and more today, companies are becoming partners with other companies as technologies converge and it becomes clear that no one company can do it all. In such an environment, it can make perfect sense for the CEOs of two major partners to share the stage and the spotlight. The sharing in itself becomes an event, in addition to the drawing power of each CEO on his or her own. Think of the three tenors. Each one a star on his own, but together, they are true worldbeaters. But think hard, because if you're going to do it, it has to work, for both of you. And it doesn't always.

Realistically, of course, few of us are in a position to demand the solo spotlight. We're going to have to do the panels, pay our dues. But we still have the power to insist on getting our fair share. So the first question is, is it worth your time and effort to share the spotlight?

Often the answer will be yes. But to get to yes you have to answer even more questions. For example, who are the *confirmed* other speakers? Not invited. Confirmed. You don't want any surprises if and when you turn up on show day to see a tableful of B list substitutes.

Not only that, you want to have a pretty good idea of what your copanelists are likely to say, their biases and where they may clash with your version of the truth. So a little research is in order, even if you know your cospeakers from long experience. Organization Web sites are great places to find previous speeches and presentations by these folks to give you an idea not only of their substance but also their style. Your networks of contacts can also fill in some blanks as to the effectiveness of the other guy's pitch. Bottom line: Know your competition. Minimize surprise.

You Want to Do It When?

Contrary to popular belief, the Edsel was not a lousy car. Quite the opposite. It was well built, well designed (design of course being a subjective thing), and big enough for a good-sized family of the late 1950s. But it went down as one of the great product failures in business history. Why? Because people were turning away from the Bulgemobiles of the Eisenhower era. They were ready for the Mustangs of the world—small, nimble, and flexible enough to be a great second car for Mom to taxi the kids around and for eldest son to soup up into a muscle car. The lesson of the Edsel was not "lousy car." Goodness knows, there have been enough of those, even post-Edsel. The lesson of the Edsel was "bad timing."

As in product introductions, timing is a big thing in deciding whether to give a speech or not. That invitation may be for a date right at the end of your quarter, and you're just not too sure how that quarter will turn out. Would you accept? I wouldn't. Too much uncertainty. Too much risk that the buzz around your appearance would be on your organization's results, not on your speech.

On the other hand, you get an invitation to give a talk right around the time of a planned innovation or deal involving your organization. If you can get the two to coincide, you've got yourself a built-in platform and a very strong additional element of the overall PR tactical rollout. It's like giving your speech an after-life, enabling you to market it to all sorts of influencers as not just another tirade but as actual news that is surely of great interest to the recipient.

Be Ready to Stand Out

When all the logistics look good, as does the topic, your expertise in it, and the timing of the event, there is still one fundamental question to ask yourself. It's about your mind-set.

You know the old line about the proud mother and the uncoordinated kid in the third line of the drill corps: "Everybody's out of step except my son John." There's a place for conformity, several of them in fact. A drill team is one of them. It just looks better if everyone lifts his or her right foot at the same time. A balance sheet works better if everyone adheres to the rules, defines things the same way, and reports them in some recognizable order. Our roads are safer when everyone conforms to the idea that a red light means stop.

But conformity brings with it some heavy luggage, baggage that is too much to carry if your objective is to define a distinct brand for yourself. For conformity inevitably involves a cloak of anonymity. Ever heard of a renowned Amish individual? Neither have I. The sect's brand is totally a function of the group, not of any individual within it. Anonymity cannot be your goal if you are to get the most out of a speaking opportunity. You've made an investment of time, money, and reputation. And so conformity must be on your personal "don't" list. Your objective is to stand out.

Clearly, this is one of the most difficult issues you will face when it comes to any speaking opportunity. Human beings are tribal people and like to wear tribal emblems to show they belong. There's a lot of lip service paid to wanting to stand out. But deep down, most people are happy when their heads don't break the horizon, as they used to say in the foxhole.

I always chuckle when I see the serious nonconformists that make up a part of my daughters' school population. Blue hair. Black clothes. Chains. Black eye makeup. The Goth look. Symbol of nonconformity. But if you want to belong you'd better not wear a turquoise shirt with your safety pin lip piercing. You'd better conform to our view of the world.

Kids are no different than we are. The dark suits, white shirts, and dark ties of the golden age of IBM may be gone, but the pressure to look, act and talk like everyone else in your circle is no less strong, no less pervasive. Think khaki. One could argue that our heightened awareness of what is or is not politically correct has placed even tighter fences around our putative individuality. The fear of giving offense prompts many speakers to choose pablum over provocative—and live with the polite applause that ensues.

Let's be clear: Being memorable on the podium does not mean having a license to slam the opposite sex, deny the Holocaust, or ridicule rodeo clowns. It doesn't mean addressing a business audience while sporting Sk8tr Boi baggy pants and an Alan Iverson ink job all over your upper torso. It does mean using other tools at your disposal to break the mold, to run at least a little bit contrary to convention.

There are many ways to do that. But first, you have to want to. You have to understand that you and your talk are just a small part of the visual and aural stimuli that are coming at your audience—certainly that day, but even while you're talking. Maybe they're thinking about a news item they saw that morning, or an over-coffee conversation with their partner, or kid. Maybe the room's too hot. Maybe they've got an annual physical coming up and a healthy fear of being probed in odd places. Maybe they're thinking of the pile of work on their desks, or an idea that a previous speaker floated.

You have to cut through all that. You have to go against the tide of conventionality. Otherwise, you'll be forgotten. And the return on your investment will be zilch, for you, your organization, and your cause.

Unfortunately, a lot of people equate standing out on the podium with showy gimmicks. And gimmicks, unless they're handled right and unless they have some obvious and compelling connection to your main message, have a better than 50–50 chance of reducing your credibility. You might be remembered, but for the wrong reasons.

It's a trap we all fall into from time to time. For a big internal sales rally one year, we arranged for our CEO to kick off the event with just such a gimmick. He loved Arthur C. Clarke's Third Law: "Any sufficiently advanced technology is indistinguishable from magic." So my colleague and I thought, in our cleverness, "Let's get Bob to do a magic trick to open up his motivational speech." Well, Bob was skeptical. Somewhere inside a voice was telling him he was no magician and this was a little bit too far removed from where he could credibly be. But we persevered, and he trusted us.

We found a magician who would teach him the rings trick—you know, where you have two or three steel rings that, despite the fact that they have no apparent breaches in the metal, can be joined and separated at will by the prestidigitator. Sworn to secrecy about how the trick is done, Bob took lessons from a bona fide magician. And he practiced diligently. But it took enormous amounts of time, a precious commodity for him. As well, being a perfectionist, he could see in the mirror that, although he could do the trick, he could not match the skill and showmanship he knew people had seen in professionals. So his confidence level was low going in.

In the event, he did the trick. But it fell flat. Perhaps it was that he had focused so fully on doing the stupid trick that he had nothing left to deliver the message. More likely, it was that the trick was so far removed from the message that it failed to connect with the audience. Not a shining moment for yours truly.

Another time at a major industry conference on the West Coast, I convinced Bob to go with no audiovisual backup. "Just talk and let your presence be your a/v." It's a sermon I often preach. Bob was comfortable with this until the night before the event, when we got wind of the plan of a competitor CEO who was to speak after Bob. The competitor, it seems, was going to enter on a Harley-Davidson. What's more, they had a video already shot showing the Hogmaster on the road on his way to the venue. Of course, the video was timed so that as it ended, the audience would hear the roar of the bike offstage and the CEO, live, would burst through the curtains on his bike to tumultuous applause.

Must have seemed like a good idea on paper. Admittedly it got a few laughs, but that's about all. The bike had nothing to do with what the guy talked about after stripping off his helmet and his leathers. And the audience wasn't fooled. In the postconference feedback, Bob—whose only gimmick was his words—came out ahead of the biker.

Ideally, then, the iconoclast in you will be most apparent not in gimmicks but in the substance of your content—fresh ideas, or old ones described in fresh ways. It will be your rapier-like wit, your "Aha!" anecdotes, your candor. (I almost wrote "unexpected candor," but that would be redundant, given that most of what speakers say today is so finely spun by so many wordsmiths and policy wonks that any provocative frankness has a snowball's chance in hell of surviving to the final version of the text.)

Candor is, indeed, one of the most compelling ways to break out of conventionality. It's what made Earl Spencer's eulogy for his sister, Diana, Princess of Wales, so memorable. Amid oceans of gushing of the media, the masterful pomp and circumstance of a British royal funeral, and the strictly controlled statements of the House of Windsor, Spencer stood out because he told some bold truths that everyone knew, yet no one else said.

He pilloried the jackals of the press: ". . . of all the ironies about Diana, perhaps the greatest was this: a girl given the name of the ancient goddess of hunting was, in the end, the most hunted person of the modern age." He slagged the royals and the pressures they put on Princes Harry and William. To the departed Diana, he said: "On behalf of your mother and sisters, I pledge that we, your blood family, will do all we can to continue the imaginative way in which you were steering these two exceptional young men so that their souls are not simply immersed by duty and tradition but can sing openly as you planned." Very deft, but a slag of the bluebloods nonetheless.

Most of all, Spencer captured Diana warts and all, an uncommon thing in the middle of the virtual canonization going on around the world from the moment of her death: "For all the status, the glamour, the applause, Diana remained throughout a very insecure person at heart, almost childlike in her desire to do good for others so she could release herself from deep feelings of unworthiness of which her eating disorders were merely a symptom." To stand alone and say those things in front of the world took great courage. It would have been easy to speak words of comfort, of tribute. But Spencer chose a different path and made a memorable speech.

No one expects a CEO to open the kimono that wide at a Rotary Club beanfest or the Widget Summit. But in a time when the world abounds in public relations experts who pray to the god of euphemism, a little straight talk goes a long way. If you go into it ready, and determined, to stand out. Running with the pack is safe—at least in the short run. But if someone puts you on the podium, why not take the lead?

Make or Buy

One other set of questions may cross your mind at this point. Should you assign the writing to someone else, either within your organization or a freelancer? Ideally, since the words will eventually come out of your mouth, priority should go to writing it yourself. That's what this book is all about.

But the real-world environment can make that tricky. This is why, in Appendix C, you'll find a full discussion of the pros and cons and the ups and downs of having someone ghostwrite your speech.

Saying No Is a Viable Option

Finally you're ready to say yes. You've asked the questions. You've received answers, for the most part the right ones. So what's holding you back? That's just a little voice in the back of your head saying, "It's not the right time," or "I don't know enough about widgets," or whatever.

Listen to that little voice. Don't obey it, necessarily. But listen closely. For the thing to remember is that if you do say yes, if you do get up on your hind feet and think out loud for 20 minutes, it is first and foremost you who will be the magnet for anything that goes wrong. You'll be the one who hems, haws, and stutters at the first question from the audience because you have only a general idea of the subject while the people on the other side of the spotlight have spent their lives on that one point you kind of skimmed over late one night.

You'll be the one who gets flustered when your assumed keynote turns into a late-day panel. Or when you show up with a well-thought-out philosophy piece while your competitor comes armed with barbs like a Don Rickles at a Friar's Club roast.

There will be times when you can get away with ignoring those little voices. After all, few situations are perfect, unless you orchestrate them yourself. But your personal brand and the reputation of your organization is too important to put on the line in a situation where you haven't considered every angle and eliminated as much as possible the potential for blindsides.

You have the power to shape the event to your needs. And that includes the power to say no. As Mark Twain said, "Better to shut your mouth and be thought a fool than open it and remove all doubt."

Key Points

- What's my objective for this appearance?

- Is the audience one I need to reach to meet the objective?

- If so, is this the best medium to reach them?

- Is the format right?

- Is this the best time?

- Is the time and money investment worth the return?

- What do I risk by opting out?

- Am I ready to stand out?

- Can I say no?

PART III

Before You Write a Word

To get an audience, create a disturbance.

—GAELIC MAXIM

Be Prepared

So let's recap. You've received an invitation to speak. You've determined that it's the right audience at the right time and you're the right person to make the appearance. So you're ready to get down to writing, right? Not necessarily.

Before getting down to actually sullying the pristine page . . . or computer screen . . . with words, there is more to do. Start by reminding yourself that your goal is to be memorable. Then set out to make it so.

It's not as if you have to reinvent the wheel. In fact, just keeping your eyes and ears open is a good beginning. Because you just never know where that next nugget will come from.

Emulate. Emulate. Emulate.

I expect you'll be glad to know that Oral Roberts University has successfully come through its trial of tough times in the early 1990s. The self-styled charismatic university saw its enrollment decline, piled up a huge debt, even had to close the City of Faith medical facility. But all that's turned around. The former hospital is now an office complex, on top of which sits a transmitter for the ORU television station. The student population has returned to mid-1980s levels. And its athletic teams once again have Division I status in the NCAA. Can there be any stronger piece of evidence to prove that ORU is back? I think not.

So what? Well, the leaders of this university say it was "founded in the fires of evangelism and upon the unchanging precepts of the Bible." I say it was founded on the power of a single, extraordinary speechmaker—Oral Roberts. He was one of a band of men and women who have raised untold gazillions of dollars almost entirely on the strength of their ability to use the spoken word to separate men and women from their cash. And Oral Roberts University is perhaps the most graphic physical symbol of that power.

Leave aside the theology. Leave aside the ethics of preying upon the fears and illnesses and troubles of the unwashed masses—and I mean that almost literally. Leave aside the slicked-back hair that belongs on a snake-oil salesman, and the expensive shiny suits. And look at the results. So-called ministries that run multimillion-dollar budgets, employ thousands, build great cathedrals of glass. Boil it all down, and those results come from one thing: the ability of these people to speak, to enlist the support of their audience, in the tent and at home over the television. That is powerful speaking.

It's something my father taught me. He was an early riser, even on weekends, and often I would find him in front of the television on Sunday morning, watching Billy Graham or Oral Roberts talk. Just talk.

Although not a religious person, Dad had been raised in a strict Swedish Baptist family—no dances, no whiskey except for medicinal purposes, and titillating stories of the young bucks in the town grabbing the front-row seats for the full-immersion baptisms of the nubile teenage girls. So he was culturally predisposed to listen to the hellfire-and-brimstone guys on the airwaves. But it was not a theological interest he took. He was watching the performance, seeing what he could learn. For he too was a speechwriter and coach for senior executives.

It's a habit I've picked up, and not a few Sundays mornings I will, rather than go to church, flip on the tube to check out my personal favorite, Jimmy Swaggart. Has there ever been a guy with a name that fits him better? Swaggart, a guy who has had incredible success despite being caught with a hooker in a cheap hotel. Why? Because he puts on a show, not in a *Lion King/Matrix* special effects extravaganza sort of way. But a show nevertheless. He swaggers back and forth across the stage, using every trick in his actor's repertoire: the floppy Bible, the glasses that he dons and takes off as the text demands, his flowing hair, his body language, hunching over, leaning back, even his sweat. They all say "commitment," "passion."

When was the last time a speaking coach told you to wander all over the stage? Wave your hands? Chew on the earpiece of your glasses? Swipe your fevered brow with a handkerchief? A handkerchief, for goodness sake! Who uses those anymore? More likely the advice is to stand straight or people will get seasick, and don't move away from the podium. Keep your arm movements to a minimum or people will think you're slightly off—or more. Don't let them see you sweat.

Oh really? Now, lest I be misunderstood, I do not believe that everyone has it in them to deliver a speech like Jimmy Swaggart. But in his approach to the podium, there are things we can and should learn, such as:

- Your body is a powerful prop.

- Movement can add drama, can break down the wall between the audience and the speaker.

- Tone and inflection . . . and pauses . . . add color and emphasis.

Swaggart's sermons are full of pauses. He appears to contemplate in silence. Or he wipes the sweat from his face. Pushes back his greasy long hair that has come all askew as he made his last vehement point. He gives the audience time to think, to anticipate. He starts low and slow, then builds. He tells stories—true or not doesn't really matter—that enable him to connect with the audience on a human level. All these tricks and more he and his counterparts perform. And they make very good money at it. On the strength of that performance.

Some of the greatest speakers of our time have borrowed liberally from these evangelists. Bill Clinton's speeches were full of the ebb and flow of the great preachers of his southern heritage. Martin Luther King, Jr., too, didn't move too far from his roots. His "I Have a Dream" speech has the palpable rhythms and cadence, the pounding repetition that punctuates so many fundamentalist services of worship. The language is right out of the liturgy: words such as "sacred obligations," "righteousness"; phrases such as "now is the time to rise from the dark and desolate valley of segregation." And then he begins his infamous litany: "I have a dream," he begins slowly, "that one day this nation will rise up and live out the true meaning of its creed—we hold these truths to be self-evident that all men are created equal."

Then he picks up steam: "I have a dream that one day on the red hills of Georgia the sons of former slaves and the sons of former slave owners will be able to sit down together at the table of brotherhood." You can almost hear the first tentative "Amens."

Then there's more. "I have a dream that my four little black children will one day live in a nation where they will not be judged by the color of their skin but by the content of their character." Amen, brother.

And again: "I have a dream today!" Followed quickly by another and another until he quotes the Bible and dreams of a day when every valley shall be exalted, every hill and mountain shall be made low, the rough places plain and the crooked places straight. Then to the climax, again repeated over and over again: Let freedom ring. Ten times in quick succession.

And finally the close: ". . . in the words of the old Negro spiritual, 'Free at last, free at last. Thank God Almighty, we are free at last.'" Now that is what I call a great speech. And it uses the techniques of great speakers King had seen, had grown up with.

The point is not that any speaker today, in particular a business person, should be citing African American spirituals. Rather, it is to be alive to the techniques that other speakers use to connect with their audience. Evangelists are easy to access because they're all over the television at certain times of the week. And, because so much of what they do is larger than life, their technique is oftentimes less subtle.

But the airwaves are filled with other opportunities to watch speakers, from presidential addresses to the droning legislative assemblies on public access channels. With hundreds of conferences going on around the country every day, it's also not that hard or expensive to see people in the flesh. In a day at a conference, you can easily see twenty or more speakers—and you can learn from each of them. In most cases, you'll learn what not to do. But that's okay.

You remember the old story about Thomas Edison. When he was asked if he was disappointed that he had failed yet again to find the right filament for his fledgling electric light, he said: "Not at all. I haven't failed . . . I've succeeded in finding 1,000 filaments that do not work." (Or words to that effect, since he hadn't yet invented the tape recorder.) Then again, there's always the chance you'll see the odd speaker who gets it, who breaks through the haze of mind-numbing conformity to connect with you and the rest of the audience. And from him or her, you can learn a great deal.

So to sum up, relentlessly check out other speakers. Make note of the best and the worst. Adapt what's best for you and ignore the rest.

Keep a "Good Stuff" File

As I write this, I am sitting almost literally knee-deep amidst four overflowing file folders. Each is labeled "Good Stuff" with ascending number descriptors I through IV. Let's just dip into one and see what we can find.

Here's a piece from a university alumni magazine on the impact on the economy of a reduction in government funding of research and development (or research and innovation as it is morphing into these days)—from 1994.

Here's a hand-scrawled note, my handwriting, no source or date: "The Industrial Revolution ended in 1992 when Microsoft stock value higher than GM." Then there's a reprint of an article from *Forbes* magazine by George Gilder on the future of newspapers in a digital world. Then a graph clipped from a newspaper showing how quickly households adopted various electronic gadgets. Then a long feature from *The Economist* on the seven marvels of the modern world. Then lots more articles from *The Economist,* on the world after communism, on physicist Richard Feynman, on transnational companies.

But there are also curiosities. An article from *The New York Times* on predictions that have failed to come true—most famously, perhaps, when the manager of the Grand Ole Opry said to Elvis Presley, "You ain't goin' nowhere, son. You ought to go back to drivin' a truck."

Scads of trivia culled from sundry newsletters:

- Only four of one hundred dissatisfied customers will ever complain via letter or phone call.

- The earliest time about which scientists can speak with any confidence is one one-hundredth of a second after Zero Time (the Big Bang).

- The Burgess Shale, a massive fossil deposit in Alberta, contained 30 arthropods. Today there are only three. Conclusion: The story of life is not a broadening of options but quite the opposite.

- Western Union once turned down the chance to buy Alexander Graham Bell's key patents for $100,000.

- The average tenure for a company listed on the S&P 500 in the 1920s and '30s was more than sixty-five years. Today it is about ten.

- Wal-Mart is the biggest company in the world.

- Nokia, the world's largest make of cell phones, began life as a wood pulp and rubber boot maker.

- In 1971, about 343,000 Americans offered some sort of legal services. By the end of the 1980s, the number was close to 1 million, just under 300 percent growth at the same time the population was growing by 20 percent.

Page after page of newspaper clippings, Internet trivia, magazine features—all grist for the mill even if only to act as a catalyst for an innovative theme. Sometimes they are actual clippings or photocopies, sometimes just handwritten notes. All are chucked in together in no particular order except the point in time when something about the article attracted me. Oftentimes, there are more formal notes, for when I read a book—nonfiction that is—I read with a pen in hand and a pad of quarter-inch graph paper beside me (it helps me keep my bullets and subbullets lined up.)

No matter the subject. If it catches your eye, sometime, somewhere there may be the opportunity to see if it will catch the ear of your audience. That it will make the connection you want to make. Case in point: The January 6, 1990, issue of *The Economist* contained a brief story on the accelerating pace of biological extinction. Now I'm no a tree-hugger, nor do I work for clients who are involved in environmental or biological issues in anything but a cursory way. But something caught my eye, and I cut out the page because it contains one of my favorite anecdotes of all time. One seemingly tailor-made for our age. One that, if it weren't true, you couldn't make up.

The story contained a single paragraph about the Stephens Island wren. This was a flightless bird that lived on one island—Stephens Island, no surprise—near New Zealand. The species thrived happily in its isolation for eons. It had no predators and thus no need to learn how to fly. Then, in the 1890s, someone built a lighthouse on the island. In those days, of course, there were no automatic lighting systems, so a human lighthouse keeper moved in. For company, this particular lighthouse keeper brought a cat—a single, domestic cat. And this cat immediately took to doing what cats have done since the dawn of time.

Unfortunately, the Stephens Island wrens were sitting ducks, so to speak. They had no experience of such an enemy and consequently no adaptive ability. It was such easy pickin's for the cat, in fact, that within a few years, the Stephens Island wren achieved the dubious distinction of being the only species every driven into extinction by a single housecat.

What a great metaphor for adapting to change . . . or not. What a connection with the common human experience. Everyone knows cats. Most people have a pretty good idea what a small bird looks like, not to mention a lighthouse. Like I said, you couldn't write fiction that is this good. What's interesting to me in this age of customized search engines on the Internet is this: I would never had seen the Stephens Island wren story if I'd asked Google to come up with a metaphor for change, or enlighten me on the theory behind disruptive technologies.

It's why I almost never ask people to do research for me. Another person could have read that issue of the magazine and never have seen the reference. Just like I can read an issue of *Playboy* and never see Gore Vidal's short story. Different filters. If you're looking into the details of a specific topic, you can get someone to do it for you. But if you want that offbeat fact, that little anecdote that raises your talk out of the mundane, you have to keep your eyes and ears open all the time. Like a magpie, collect shiny bits, because you just never know.

Here's another example. If you're like me, you get a pretty constant stream of jokes and funny lists from your e-mail, happy friends and family. Most produce a quick smile, and then you push "delete." But some have something shiny about them. In this case, it was a list of oxymorons a friend sent to me a couple of years ago. You know: military intelligence, airplane food, tight slacks, sensitive guy. I stashed it in the "Wit" folder on my laptop for future reference.

Then I was asked to write a speech for a senior executive. His challenge was to transform the customer operations group from an overhead organization into, if not a profit center, at least a source of new revenue. The idea was to sell to external customers the solutions and services they'd developed for internal use. A customer operations group as a revenue source? Seemed like an oxymoron to me. And a nice place to start a speech on the unusual challenge he faced.

The point is that the search for shiny new material that makes that connection between you and your audience never ends. It's never a tidy process and, in fact, is often literally quite messy. My version of Good Stuff files may be altogether too chaotic for many more disciplined minds. But however you keep your files, you'll find them useful to poke through before you sit down to write any speech. Without exception, just exploring the files will set your mind to wandering (and wondering), often in free association. It's a perfect setting for the muse of creativity to make an appearance.

Key Points

- Study great speakers.

- Adapt the techniques that you can carry off.

- Watch how they use their bodies as a prop; their voices to create drama.

- Be a pack rat for interesting facts and thought starters.

Find the Hook

There's an energy that crackles through the room when you approach the podium to speak. The same kind of energy that fills a theater when the curtain rises. It's a moment of expectation, of anticipation, perhaps of some drama. It is not a moment to waste with conventional pleasantries. It is a time when the audience is most open to the speaker. It is your moment to hook them with an indelible first impression, like a Top 40 pop song that grabbed your teenaged heart.

So even before writing a word, it pays to spend a lot of time figuring out your hook. Your nervousness and the audience's anticipation are both human emotions. It is the perfect moment to respond with a hook that sets itself right in the imaginative center of your listeners' brains.

There are numerous ways to make that connection. In this chapter, we look at half a dozen.

The Story Hook

A properly written news story is shaped like an inverted triangle. The most important, weightiest facts go at the top of the story. Then the second most important, then the third, and so on down to the bottom of the story. It's done this way because, in daily newspapers, writers and editors are never sure until the last minute how much space they'll have to fill. Often, if the space for the story turns out to be smaller than the story is long, an inverted-triangle model makes it easy just to lop off the last couple of sentences or paragraphs to make the story fit. No harm done, as the most important part, the lead of the story, is still intact at the top.

The classic model of a speech has been likened to a set of bookends: strong and broad at the start and finish, with a bunch of stuff in the middle. In other words, there's a strong start; a middle that proves the start; and a strong finish that reiterates the start. Whoever came up with this classic model had one thing right: People do tend to remember the first thing a speaker says and the last. So why don't the bookends work?

Because the second bookend is the same as the first. You've heard it all before, not twenty minutes ago. What's more, because everybody does it, you *know* you've heard it before so you can, without guilt, nod off or check your BlackBerry for e-mail and instant messages as you kill time till the next session. In fact, I tend to think of the classic model as a circle—you end up where you started, no further along the road. And what's the point of running in circles?

That's why I advocate a speech model that looks more like this:

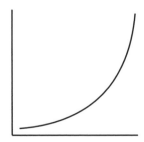

It's the classic story-telling arc, building in interest and involvement from the opening till the climax. The curtain doesn't open with the stage strewn with dead bodies. It opens with the introduction of a problem and the people who must confront this crisis. And as the actors deal with the challenge in various ways, they take the audience with them, inveigling them little by little to participate, even if just intellectually or emotionally. The tension rises as complications appear. The connection between watcher and watched strengthens until the resolution is reached. If it's a tragedy, most if not all of the star-crossed characters are dead, and we're supposed to feel a sense of catharsis, cleansed by having gone through the trauma. If it's a comedy, the boy does get the girl, laughter ensues, and a life of picket fences and darling babies beckons.

In truth, in a first-rate story, the curve is never as smooth as this. There are sharp inclines as tension mounts, and plateaus as everyone, hero and reader, catches his or her collective breath, then on to the next complication, then breather, then complication, till at last you get the resolution. But always, always, the momentum is building, not stopping to review what you already know, not heading back to where you began, but moving inexorably toward a new, higher plain.

The Power of Story

Story-telling is the most common form of entertainment. But it is also the most effective way we humans have yet devised to teach (or to learn, depending on your perspective). Its roots are impeccable. Look at one of history's greatest teachers, a fellow named Jesus, from Nazareth. Regardless of what faith you follow, if any, you cannot escape the fact that this man, through the power of his stories, has had an enormous impact on the shape of our world. His life story is an integral part of the Christian calendar: his lowly birth in humble surroundings of poor but proud craftsmen parents; his tempestuous youth, rebelling against the economic power brokers of the day; his show-stopping events, from turning water into wine to raising the dead and feeding the multitudes with a couple of bonefish and some bread. We have his mature philosophy—theology, call it what you will— and the inevitable, fatal clash with the political authorities; then the miraculous dénouement—the ascension—and the basis of a faith that has enraptured billions of people for more than two millennia. Apocryphal or not, there's no denying it's a great story, as a newspaper person might say.

Then look at the way Jesus taught, the way he enlisted support. Certainly, he lived the way he preached, and that is a powerful attractor, a brand builder par excellence. But primarily he was a story teller, and the parables he told are woven into the fabric of our lives, at least in the West: the sower and the seed, the prodigal son, the house built on rock or on sand. This last one has its echo in one of the earliest stories many of us hear as children—the Big Bad Wolf and the Three Little Pigs and their houses made of sticks, straw, or brick.

And that is the point. From our earliest stirrings as cognitive beings—that is, creatures who can react not only to physical stimuli but also to abstract ideas—we learn the lessons of life, we absorb the values of our culture through stories. Stories form the basis of our myriad faiths. Stories tell of the history of our secular communities. Stories illuminate our own ancestral roots. Stories are the most fundamental method by which we begin to make sense of our world. They help define who we are and what we think, what ideas we reject, what causes we support.

What's more, stories are the basis of most of our entertainment even in the multimedia universe of our entertainment today. Television, the movies, live theater—they're all story-telling media. X-box games are story driven. Much of the content of the Internet likewise, as billions of chatroom users and Web site owners seek to attract some eyeballs to their own stories. Certainly there are people who live for the pure gore and mayhem of a *Kill Bill,* the special effects of a *Matrix* (pick a version), or the visceral bang and crash of a Monster truck rally. But most people who don't wear their baseball caps backwards actually respond more readily—and more indelibly—to the plot thread that ties the explosions together. Why do you think the world of professional wrestling, and I use the words loosely, is less about *mano-a-mano* in the classic Greek sense of the sport and more about cartoon characters in the flesh following broad plotlines that are simple variations on ages-old morality plays? Whatever else he may be, Vince McMahon is surely a wizard of a marketer. He gets people, millions of people, to suspend their disbelief and buy into his world vision. And he knows he needs the story to make the connection.

Does it not follow, then, that modeling a speech after the structure of a story might just be an effective way to connect with the audience? Yet you rarely, if ever see it. And that's a shame, because it can really work.

Some years ago, I was lucky enough to do a couple of assignments for an executive who had figured this out. I was called in by the PR staff of Xerox Canada to prepare a speech for their new CEO. It was the first time this subsidiary had had a female CEO, the staff said, and they wanted to capitalize on that, given the egalitarian tenor of the times. Plus they really wanted to hit heavily on the fact that Xerox was changing its name, putting its new slogan ahead of the name: The Document Company—Xerox. The PR staff, thinking they were being helpful, sent me a thick package of background material, including a draft outline that emphasized the corporate messaging strategy: times of change; female leader; new name putting what we do ahead of what we're called. Yada, yada, yada.

Then I met with the executive, clearly a focused and driven woman, but one who understood the need to make a connection with those she spoke to, both one to one, and one to many. She was gracious in meeting me, and when I suggested we go over the draft outline, she was a step ahead of me: "Let's put it aside for now, and just talk about this idea I have." So she talked and I listened, and scribbled notes as fast as I could. She talked of her own story, of coming from modest roots and working hard to accomplish great things. But she talked with just as much passion about the Xerox story. And those are literally the words she used: the Xerox story.

She drew a vivid picture of this large and successful company that near the end of the 1970s had essentially fallen asleep at the switch. And in doing so, it had been overtaken by offshore competitors who were putting better products on the market for much less than Xerox could. Market share had eroded. Financial losses followed, investor confidence wavered. An unhappy trend that was building momentum until the company admitted its myopia, changed its way of thinking and operating, and recreated itself.

It is in that context, she said after talking for twenty minutes, that we have renamed our company. And in this story is a lesson for others who spend too much time reading their good reviews and not enough looking ahead at what's coming at them over the horizon.

"You have just," I said, "given your speech." And she agreed. I transcribed my notes. She made a few tweaks, and we were done. We had the Xerox parable. And here is how we connected as we got into the meat of the speech, after a bit of buttering up the audience:

> The '90s arrived about 15 years ago at Xerox—and we weren't ready.

Refreshing, even radical candor. A stark, unmodified statement that said, "Listen up. This is not going to be your usual corporate babble."

> We had literally invented a better mousetrap—the plain paper copier—and spent the '60s and '70s basking in the shortsighted kudos of Wall Street. We grew fat on the industry we'd created, selling all we could at whatever price we set.
>
> But we weren't paying attention to what was happening outside our self-imposed boundaries. We were so happy simply reproducing our success that we did nothing to capitalize on other inventions that came out of our labs— little things like personal computers, the mouse, graphical user interface.
>
> You might have heard of them—but not with a Xerox name on them.

Not only confession, here, but "Gee-I-didn't-know-that" information. You could see a real spike in the interest level in the audience when she talked about those little-known facts.

> We were so busy counting our paper profits that we failed to read the Sayonara message in our Japanese fortune cookies. Until one year our profit dropped by $1 billion, overnight, and we realized that in just five years, the Japanese had gone from zero to 40 percent market share in the industry that we had created.

A Xerox lifer, the executive shared her sense of bewilderment with the audience, inviting them to experience the lost-in-the-barrens feeling Xerox executives must have gone through at the time. Then, to bring it home, she got specific:

> They were selling their machines for what it cost us to make ours. Our benchmarks were not even in the same league. Our product lead time was twice theirs; we had ten times the assembly line rejects they did; and nine times the number of suppliers. . . .

The open kimono laid bare the problem for everyone in the room. And everyone could relate. From this nadir, the executive started to build toward a happy ending, for in a speech you pretty much always want a happy ending. She talked of a relentless focus on quality, a redefinition of what Xerox was selling—not copiers but document management. It was similar to Henry Ford's story. He didn't sell cars, he used to say. He sold mobility, freedom for everyman.

That Xerox speech was so successful for this executive that she repeated it in variations for months. From her perspective, it was a great return on her investment, both financially and in terms of building her personal brand and support for the new identity of her company. It was a story her audience of senior executives could relate to. It was also a story she could sell convincingly, because it was *her* story. She had lived through the tough times herself and could talk with authenticity about the impact. "I was there" not only gets attention, it commands respect.

That is not to say that only first-person stories are useful. Far from it. The great thing about stories is that you can usually find one that fits virtually any audience. Some have universal appeal because, in their simplicity, they capture some essence of what it is to be a human being, part of a larger world.

Know the Facts . . . but Tell the Story

One of the key tricks to connecting through story-telling is to recognize that facts are not intrinsically interesting or particularly illuminating. Someone has to marshal those facts, put context around them, link them with a narrative, in order for them to be memorable.

Think of it this way. People spend more time reading biographies and novels than they do reading almanacs or tidal tables. Why? Because the *story* knits together facts—and sometimes fancy—in a pattern that is more easily digested and internalized by the human brain. Many novels are brimful of facts, but they're presented as important drivers of place, atmosphere, character, or plot. They are not the end, but a means.

Yet speakers often will present lists of facts as if this somehow creates a memorable image in the audience's mind. "Here's our Revenue. Here's our EBITDA and, of course, our Free Cash Flow." Doesn't work for me. Begs a big "So what?" Needs a narrative around it to put those numbers in context.

This is not to say that speakers should eschew facts. Far from it. Rather it is to say that facts, especially numbers, are great to illuminate a point, but almost never are they the point. Speakers may think they're imparting material of great substance because their speech is packed with lists of facts. In fact, those lists can quickly get an audience flipping through the program to see who's next. Just remember, there's a place for a telephone book, but it isn't in a speech.

Remember, too, that different people relate in different ways to statistics. And most people have no idea how big a billion really is. So your job is to humanize the data. We know, for instance, that there are more than 400,000 tobacco-related premature deaths in the U.S. every year. Big number, but how big? Well, it's your job to connect that cold hard fact with an indelible image, and which image you choose depends on your audience demographic. For some people of a certain age, you could say that's like having the whole unwashed human mass at the first Woodstock wiped from the face of the earth. For others, frequent fliers especially, it's like having three fully-loaded 747s crash every day for a full year. Or maybe there's a city of 400,000-plus in the vicinity; imagine that as a city of the dead. There are lots of ways to imprint the image on the collective brain of the audience. To bring the fact to life; to help tell your story.

The Metaphorical Hook

Being memorable from the first moment you open your mouth means plugging into the imaginative power of the audience. An image, not a picture, is worth 10,000 words. For example, when I was very little my parents read me the story of Robin Hood from a big chapter book with no pictures. From the words alone, I developed a strong mental picture of what Robin and Little John, and especially Maid Marian, looked like. In fact, I think I had a tiny little crush on Robin's love interest, whom I saw as a raven-haired beauty not unlike Maureen O'Sullivan of *Tarzan* movie fame.

Imagine my excitement, then, when word came of *Robin Hood*, the television series. Much was made of the star, some actor I'd not heard of then—or since—but my eager anticipation was focused almost entirely on Maid Marian. Imagine, too, my disappointment to see that the actress was some bleached blonde, not at all in the image that I had conjured up for myself.

I've experienced that same sinking feeling many times now as the images I conjure in my mind while reading consistently differ from—and are usually better than—what I see when the book is translated to screen. This doesn't apply just to starlets, or even people. Often, it's the on-screen physical setting that jars my senses. Call me a dreamer, but I believe that's a pretty common experience.

There's no question that a wonderful photograph can have an impact far greater than any 10,000 words. The single man confronting the Tiananmen Square tanks comes to mind. Marilyn Monroe's dress billowing over the air vent, too. But I haven't seen too many business photos that stay in my memory.

The fact is that the theaters of our minds are often much richer, and certainly much more personal, than the theaters of the local multiplex. And a good speaker can use that common experience to create powerful, personalized images in the minds of the audience—images that are compelling enough in themselves to make the speech memorable.

Take this example. One day my boss called me into his office to discuss an important speech he had to deliver a few weeks hence. Now this was the corner office on the top floor of the nine-story suburban head office of a major telecommunications equipment manufacturer. Although the building was beside a sixteen-lane highway and across from an international airport, it was the first structure in a new commercial park and was therefore still surrounded by cornfields.

My boss and I chatted for a minute or two about the opportunity and what general theme he might want to pursue. Relatively quickly, he decided he wanted to address the issue that technology was getting too complex for people to understand. His take was that although telecommunications technology was getting more and more complex, its main purpose was to make life simpler by making it easier for people to stay in touch with one another. Simplicity out of complexity.

That's a great theme, and one that remains relevant in a world of convergent communications technologies some 15 years later. It was a theme, too, that included the submessage that since our company had a good idea of what was happening at the 50,000-foot level, we'd also be the best option for operating down in the trenches where the machines were built and the connections made.

Without doubt, it was a somewhat complex and ethereal theme. We agreed that we needed to capture it in a way that made it instantly and intuitively obvious so that the audience would understand not only what was happening in technology but also see that we were the best people to deliver on its promise. In short, we needed a hook, and for fifteen minutes or so we kicked around some ideas, none of which caught fire for either of us.

Then, as people do when they're stuck for ideas or something to say, we both happened to look out the window at the same time. And there, not twenty feet from the pane of glass, with wings outstretched, hovered a beautiful adult red-tailed hawk, soaring on the updraft of the west wind that swooshed across the expanse of the airport till it hit our building. The hawk's piercing black eyes were tightly focused on the field some ninety feet below him until, with an almost imperceptible dip of one wing, he was off, shooting down to the ground where, with talons extended, he swooped once, emerging with a dumbstruck—and doomed—field mouse.

The boss and I looked at each other in one of those Eureka! moments and said, "That's it. That's our hook." It was the biological complexity of the hawk—its different systems for sight, mobility, snatching—all coming together to make simpler the fundamental need to hunt for food. In the same way, complex telephony technology was coming together to make simpler the fundamental human need to communicate.

Talk about a common experience. Who hasn't watched a hawk making lazy circles in the sky as it hunts? Who can't instantly conjure up in the mind's eye the image of a bird of prey? We took it as a sign and built the speech around that metaphor, although we changed the hawk to a falcon since the word *hawk* still had some negative post-Vietnam's connotations. But that didn't matter. The image would remain the same in the audience's perception, whether falcon, hawk, or eagle. Whatever the individual's perception, it would have the essential elements of the theme: intricacy, power, simplicity of purpose.

We didn't need a slide with the picture of a hawk on it; in fact, I would argue that a slide would have made the image less compelling, imposing an external definition on an image that was more powerful if it remained in the mind's eye of each listener. For years people who had seen the speech, or read it after, referred to it as the "Falcon speech." It was an image that caught in their memory and, as long as it was there, there was a chance that they would remember at least the speaker, if not his theme.

Another example, same industry, different speaker. This time, the boss wanted a fresh take on convergence, and especially the synergies that the convergence of various communications technologies would bring to people in general. Again, part of his objective was to calm the fears of technophobes who saw the evolution of various technologies as in some way threatening to their comfortable way of life.

Now there are no greater clichés in the technology industry than "convergence" and "synergy." So this executive's desire was to find some new way to talk about these concepts, which, although trite, were nonetheless true and gaining in prominence virtually every day. So we wracked our brains and came up empty, until, that is, we considered the time of year and the venue.

The speech was to be made in December. The venue was Ottawa, which is, except for Moscow, the coldest national capital in the world. The weather in Ottawa, they say, is ten months of snow and ice and two months of lousy sledding. What do you need in Ottawa in winter? Comfort food. What's a good comfort food? Stew. What's stew? A conglomeration of different foods all boiled up together into a meal that is greater than the sum of its parts—convergence and synergy. Voila! A common experience that conjured up an image that fit every part of the theme.

So with a few words, you can establish an immediate rapport with your audience, not just a laugh thanks to another golf joke, but a true connection based on a shared human experience. And that's a big step toward being memorable.

Another Use of the Metaphorical Hook

This is how a senior high-tech executive opened his keynote speech to the World Congress on Gifted and Talented Education in the early 1990s, about the time that Chaos theory began to have prominence.

> Four months ago last Tuesday, a young female butterfly beat her wings quickly as she soared in the calm air over Hong Kong.
> The tiny air currents the butterfly's wings set in motion grew as they encountered other forces, evolving into the weather system that has plagued the Mississippi Valley this summer.

At least that's the way the theory goes. A single butterfly's flapping wings can set in motion a chain of events that has significant impact months later and thousands of miles away.

The theory is called the Butterfly Effect, and it's one of the more poetic elements of the new science of chaos.

Although I doubt we'll ever have enough meteorologists to prove it conclusively, the theory possesses a certain logic that appeals to engineers like myself, and other people who spend their lives studying cause and effect.

More than that, the Butterfly Effect speaks eloquently to a number of important ideas that are relevant to your discussions here today.

First, small changes can have gigantic repercussions, even within huge systems.

Second, the effects of change are difficult to predict—just ask any weatherman. And third, and most important, individuals have enormous power to make change, whether they know it or not.

Location, Location, Location

Where you are is not only something you have in common with the audience. It can also be a source of the "Aha!" moment. There is nothing more immediate to an audience than its physical surroundings. By that I mean everything from the size and shape of the room, the view out the window, the amenities of the hotel, the sights of the city, right down to the comfort of the chair.

Location is tangible and in your face, and as such it can be an exceptionally compelling hook for a speech because you can be confident that it is a shared human experience for everyone in the room. And it's happening right now. Every touring musical act I've ever seen knows this, because they all include a "Hello, [your city here]" in their patter. But few, if any, really get it—really show that they know that Toledo *is* actually a different city than Birmingham, and not just another arena where they get off the tour bus.

Everyone likes to hear their hometown praised by visitors, and with a little bit of research—say ten minutes on the Internet—it's easy to come up with a nifty little fact that lets the locals know you've done more than localize a canned talk. And if the tidbit is interesting enough, it wakes up others in the audience who, like everyone else, are always looking for something novel, some bit of trivia to grease the conversational skids at the coffee break or over dinner.

But here's the trick: Make it connect with your theme. Otherwise it will seem like the mandatory opening golf joke that has nothing to do with the state of the insurance industry. Here's an example of what I mean.

On one occasion, the president of a major manufacturer was asked to address a conference of key fund-raisers for the United Way. The organizers wanted the standard "Let's go, Team" motivational yawner, only louder and longer because this year, given a real slump in giving, they needed to go the extra mile, give 110 percent, [insert your cliché here.] The executive, who had made the charity one of his main community priorities, wanted to challenge the leaders to go beyond what they had ever done before. "It's as if," he said when briefing the writer, "they're always thinking about the way things have worked in the past. They can't seem to get beyond that mind-set, and it's a real barrier to getting any sort of tangible improvement in results."

His objective was to make them feel comfortable with radical change. Make them understand that the barriers they were erecting between themselves and new, better ways to raise money were artificial. The hurdles they had to jump were man-made, and if men could make them, men could also tear them down and find their way to more effective fund-raising territory. Fairly esoteric stuff. The challenge? Make it real, make it palpable.

It so happened that the speech was to be given in Windsor, Ontario, across the Detroit River from—you guessed it—Detroit. Not only that, but the room in which the speech was scheduled had a view of the Motor City skyline across the river, one of the more spectacular views one can get in the flat midsection of this continent.

One of the interesting things about Windsor—critics might say the only interesting thing about Windsor—is that it is the only city in Canada that lies south of the United States. That's right. When the audience for this speech was looking out over the Detroit River, they were looking north. Now in the great frozen north called Canada, one just never expects to look north and see America. It never happens, except in Windsor. It's a new perspective for people, especially visitors to the city, and as such it lends itself perfectly to a thematic talk about seeing things from a new perspective.

So, part one of the theme was "Take a new perspective on an old problem." But there was another element to this location hook. Right down the middle of the Detroit River runs an international border. On one side, the northern side, it's the home of the land of the brave, where freedom rings and citizens have the pursuit of happiness enshrined in their rights. On the southern side, it's America Lite, similar but incontrovertibly different, where the loftiest goal is not happiness but peace, order, and good government.

Like most borders, at least in our part of the world, you can't see it. But it is there, put there by people who decided the upper part of North America should be split into two countries (not counting those Québecois who would opt for three). Here was a natural thoroughfare—a river—with boats crossing it regularly, with a bridge over it and a tunnel under it. Yet human beings had decided it would be something quite different—a barrier. You could get through it, over it, or under it, but you had to jump through a couple of hoops first.

It was an easy leap from there to a call to action that said, "Look, the things you've done in the past to raise funds had their uses, but they are an artificial barrier to new, more effective ways to get the job done. Just like that border out there, they are a figment of someone's imagination. Our minds built the barriers. Our minds can tear them down. And the clients of the United Way, our neighbors, friends, and families, will be better off because of it."

Because of the location, because it worked thematically, it was a memorable speech. The leadership moved the United Way to a record year, and the speaker's personal brand as an imaginative and caring leader was reinforced.

But location isn't always about the region or city you're speaking in. It can be much more granular. Let me give you a couple of related examples.

In the late 1980s, the leader of one branch of Nortel Networks, then known as Northern Telecom, decided he wanted to put some teeth into the company's ongoing rhetoric about improving education. Northern was well known as a thought leader on technical education in those days as its voracious growth absorbed newly minted engineers by the thousands every year. Despite the ready job market, however, engineering faculties had trouble attracting students, especially women. And science and math courses at the secondary school level were also becoming more sparsely populated, again particularly by females.

So, as part of an overall campaign to promote science and math courses in schools at all levels, this particular executive came up with an idea. Step 1 was to identify fifty to one hundred schoolteachers who were being innovative and making a palpable difference in the classroom. Step 2 was to bring them together for a week in the summer at a university to learn more about technology from Northern personnel and from each other, and to recharge their batteries, knowing that there were other classroom pioneers out there. And have some fun doing it.

Because it was his idea, the president wanted to address these gatherings at some point during the week. In the first year of the program, this was to be at a gala dinner at the start of the week at the university. I struggled with this speech at first because (1) we'd done a lot of education speeches in the previous couple of years and it all felt like it had been said before, and (2) because as much as we wanted to take credit for this program, we wanted to modestly let someone else say how great an idea it was. What exactly did I want him to say to people for them to take away with them? What was the call to action? What was the point?

Education is good? Zzzzzzzzzzzzzzzzzzzzzzzzzzzzzzzz!!!

I'd gone through a few nondescript drafts when, one afternoon about ten days before D-Day (delivery day), a colleague who was in charge of the logistical arrangements phoned me in a panic.

"The room's too small," she said. "They made a mistake, double-booked the room we wanted, and now we've been bumped to a couple of adjoining meeting rooms in the engineering faculty. We've got 120 people coming, and the rooms only hold 100—so you're off the dinner invite list."

Well, you can imagine my dismay. I've never met a dinner I didn't like, unless you count that one in the basement of the Seoul

Hilton where no one could help me understand what exactly it was we were eating.

"We're uninviting a few more too, so we'll be able to squeeze in. But how do I tell the boss?" The boss was a man not known for his patience. He bragged about it, in fact. He, rightly, liked things to be just so, especially when Northern was the host. This did not sound like one of those times he'd be happy.

I mulled all this over the rest of the day and into the evening—in fact, into the late-night walk with the dog around the block. "Education is good. You're great educators. Room's too small." It was like a mantra chanted over and over till, while Lindy continued to mark his 400th tree of our little stroll, it hit me. (Not Lindy—he'd exhausted his supply around tree #78.) What hit me was the Idea—the crux of the speech.

Turn the problem into a virtue. The point of the speech was that not only was the room too small physically, it was also too small metaphorically because society needed to create hundreds and thousands more teachers like these champions if we were to meet the demands of the information age for knowledge workers. It would look almost as if we'd planned to have too small a meeting room when the CEO stood up and told his guests that they represented the pioneers of a new kind of educator, and that Northern was committed to making sure we needed bigger and bigger rooms in subsequent years.

A short, simple, and tangibly effective speech. Every listener knew the room was too small because they'd been bumping elbows and more all evening. But there was a special intimacy forming during the dinner because of it, an intimacy that was extended immeasurably when the CEO stood up and admitted the obvious. The room was too small. (By the way, I listened and watched from the doorway, having fortified myself with a Big Mac beforehand.)

Interestingly, the next year we had the opposite problem, but the same theme. With a new crop of super teachers on hand, we went to a different university. This time, the CEO's address was scheduled to take place at a luncheon at the end of the week. The location: the VIP lounge at a 36,000-seat football stadium. The room was great, my organizing colleague assured me. "It's huge. It can seat 500 people probably."

"Okay," I thought out loud, "now we're talking this room is too big."

"No, no," she replied. "It will be okay. We can make it smaller with buffers and flowers and stuff."

Well, I was sort of convinced but I wanted to make sure, so I phoned the stadium myself. All seemed in order, so I got down to thinking about the speech, searching for something that would top the previous year's success.

At first, location didn't seem to be a workable approach. But then a couple of other questions came to my mind, again while I was walking the dog. The next day I called the stadium administration again.

"What's this room normally used for?"

"Well, it's where our season ticket holders can come and watch the game and have a comfortable seat and drink a few beers or cocktails, whatever."

"So it overlooks the field?"

"Yep. Big old floor-to-ceiling windows the width of the room. 'Course we'll have the curtains closed during the speech so no one will be distracted from your boss's speech."

"Hmmm. Tell me one more thing. Will there be anything on in the stadium during the speech? Any event? Even a practice?" After asking me to wait while he checked, my contact disappeared for a couple of minutes. When he came back, he confirmed that there would be no one on the field or in the stands during the luncheon.

"Perfect," I said, then explained what I wanted to happen.

When we all arrived at the stadium on the day of the event, everything was as it should have been. The room was huge, but a smaller space had been set aside with planters and buffers, perfect for the 120 people invited to the lunch. Behind the lectern was a wall of curtains, hiding the floor-to-ceiling windows.

Once the rubber chicken was being dealt with by the digestive juices of 120 stomachs, the CEO rose to speak. He started quietly, referencing that this was the second year of the program and laughing about the tiny room the previous year. "Different place, same issue this year," he said, and as he did so the curtains automatically swept open to reveal the expanse of the stadium turf and row upon row of empty seats.

"We have a roomful of great teachers here again this year, and that's terrific. But," he added as he gave a Vanna White sweep of the arm to the scene behind him, "but what we need to do is fill up those seats with great teachers." Even the accountant side of him, he said, would be thrilled to fork out the rent for the whole stadium in ten or fifteen years if those present—and like-minded people everywhere—could generate that many outstanding educators. After that, the standing O was something of an anticlimax.

It is not every day that normal people get to see a great sports stadium absolutely empty. That was neat. But to connect it with his theme, that was a memorable speech. Of course, he was preaching to the choir. But he made himself—and his company— memorable. He made a vision real. He immeasurably improved the brand in that twenty minutes, and more than recouped the company's investment in the program. And what did it take? The cost of a couple of long-distance phone calls. And some insight into the theatrical possibilities of even the most mundane speech opportunity.

The Location Hook

This speech was given by the president of a major high-tech firm to United Way leaders in Windsor, Ontario. The objective: encourage the leaders to innovate in their fund-raising efforts to overcome an anticipated shortfall due to economic pressures.

I must admit I feel a bit intimidated this morning. Maybe that's natural in a room full of people who put such an extraordinary amount of time and talent into helping others.

More likely, it's because I've always left Sunday morning sermons to others, people with better connections if you know what I mean.

So I don't propose to preach today, although I do want to share with you some thoughts on what I see happening around us.

When I was a younger man—not that much younger—my wife and I would pile our children into the family car and drive to California for vacations.

The first time, I told my son that we'd be crossing the border at Windsor/Detroit. He didn't know what a border was, so I explained that it is a line between two countries. In this case, it's a line right down the middle of the Detroit River.

Well, he was awfully disappointed when we crossed the Ambassador Bridge. "I can't see the line, Dad," he said. "No," I told him. "It's just a man-made line. It's imaginary."

Many of you dined and danced on the shore of that

imaginary line last night. And some of you, I'm sure, got an even closer look at it from a cruise boat.

That river may be the busiest international waterway in the world. But the fact remains that we—human beings—have made it an artificial barrier.

When my parents were growing up, the barrier was high—at least in theory. The fastest boats on the river belonged to the bootleggers who used the technology available at the time to poke holes in Prohibition.

When my children were growing up, the barrier had come down to a large extent, and the river became famous for the hydroplane races.

Today, as I continue to grow up, the boats that really define the river for me are the freighters of industry as we see the barrier redefined once again with the Canada-U.S. free trade agreement.

The barrier is what we make it. The line is imaginary.

The same is true for most of the limits we place on ourselves and our organizations. And that's really what I want to talk about today: breaking down the old barriers, crossing the imaginary line.

Hook Them Through Time

On any Sunday in the latter half of his long life, my father could be found in what we called the library of our home, deeply immersed in a history of the Second World War, or snoozing in the chair with the book open across his chest. He was entitled. After all, he'd long ago finished his five-mile dawn hike, his ritual bundling of the week's newspapers, and his cottage cheese and toast lunch. The library walls were floor-to-ceiling hardcover books, thick and intimidating, mostly about History with a capital H, and mostly about World War II.

In my early years, I grew up with the perception that World War II was remote in time from my peaceful reality. It belonged to another world. It's probable that my perception was fed by the fact that every Sunday afternoon, while Mom busied herself in the kitchen with the roast, Dad would tune in Walter Cronkite's "World at War" television series. The grainy, jumpy black-and-white newsreels were a far cry from the Technicolor Lone Ranger movies we'd been to Saturday afternoon. Interesting, but about as connected with my world as the Egyptian mummies in the museum.

Then, one day, I had one of those epiphanies that stops you in your tracks, at least mentally. I remember thinking, all of a sudden, that WWII was not some distant event. It had ended just seven years before I was born. I don't remember when it was that this lightning bolt struck my thick cranium, but I do remember that I could recall things that had happened seven years before that time. And they seemed to have happened yesterday. That is what it must have been like for my parents when I was born. The war must have been a fresh memory.

Something else occurred to me at about that time in my life. I remember a small item in the paper announcing that the last veteran of the Civil War had died. Civil War? That was way back. And someone who had been in the war was alive? At least until recently? I was amazed. I believe the person in question had been just a boy, a drummer or a flag bearer in the War Between the States. And he'd lived to well over 100 years old. But it gave me a little thrill to think my world today had such a direct link with something that truly was History, with someone who had been alive at the same time as such mythic figures as Abraham Lincoln and Robert E. Lee. It was a sense of continuity, of connection with a great moment in history. No question, it was a somewhat tenuous connection. But for anyone with a romantic cast of mind, that is no problem.

The reality is that our culture, our values, are shaped by history. And it is not the dry history of textbooks. It is the living history of the people in our lives, however briefly. It's like six degrees of separation with another dimension: time. It's fun to connect people to others who live at the same time through broad overlapping circles of acquaintance. But add in a time line, and there's a whole new level of connection.

An example. As kids, we played cowboys and Indians endlessly, fed by TV shows starring the likes of Roy Rogers, Gene Autry, and the Cisco Kid. We loved the action, but the connection was even stronger for me because of a friend my parents had. This man had parents, don't we all, and his parents had been scalped . . . and lived to tell the tale. I never met these poor bewigged people, but I met the man, and that was enough to let me think I had a direct connection with those horse operas I watched on the big and little screen all the time.

Another example: my own mother. This is a woman who lives in very comfortable retirement in a lovely home in one of the most affluent towns in the country. She has at her fingertips all the latest gadgets technology can devise. Yet she once traveled by covered wagon. In the 1920s, her father lost his farm in southern Alberta after consecutive years of drought and hail wiped out his crops. With nothing but a horse, a cow, a dog, and a covered wagon, Ernie Beetlestone packed up his wife, Beatrice, and their three children and headed north. For weeks they trekked, sleeping rough, surviving often only on the kindness of strangers. At one point, Ernie had to trade the dog for a gun so he could hunt to feed the family. At another point, the exhausted family was taken in for several days of rest and refreshment by a band of Blackfoot Indians. Eventually, the Beetlestones staked a homestead claim well north of Edmonton, in the Peace River country, where their first shelter was a sod hut.

The contrast between my mother's early life and her later years is a stark metaphor for the kind of change this past century has wrought. And her story has been a part of several speeches I have written. It's not just the wonders of what's happened to our world since the 1920s embodied in a tiny, feisty Irish mother. It's also a lesson about the future. If Madeline Carlson can, in the space of a lifetime, move from a covered wagon to the Internet, what will we see in our own lives? It's mind-boggling. But it's also grounded in a human story—human history, if you will, with a lower case *h*.

All of this is to make a simple point. Often, a great way to make the all-important connection with the audience is to bring to bear the historical context. We're great ones for celebrating anniversaries. Fifty years of *Playboy* magazine rates a two-hour prime-time special, for goodness' sake. Or perhaps not for goodness' sake. We're also fascinated by trivia. After all, how long has *Jeopardy* been a television staple? And history—whether the h is lower or upper case—is full of interesting tidbits of trivia.

So if an anniversary of some neat event falls on the day you're making your speech, it's a legitimate way to make the quick and lasting connection. But it goes without saying that it should have some relevance to your theme. I'm not talking about building a speech around the anniversary of the group you're talking to, or some other conventional milestone. It's probably polite to acknowledge such landmarks, but it won't make the talk memorable. Rather, I'm talking about making a new connection with history, through a piece of information that the audience is probably not aware of. Give them an "Aha!" moment, then bring it home by defining its relevance to your topic.

There are books and Worldwide Web resources that list "This Day in History" references in exhaustive detail. Most of the stuff is too obscure to be of much use. But sometimes, with a little creativity and a bit more research, you can make it work. For instance, I once had a client who was scheduled to deliver a talk about disruptive technologies on April 3. This was before the concept of disruptive technologies was part of the lexicon of the business world. But people knew about them. The old chestnut about buggy-whip manufacturers having it in for Henry Ford was well known. Of course, that's what made it an old chestnut.

I was a bit stumped for a new angle on this, so I did what I always do when the muse is playing coy. I sifted through my Good Stuff files, ransacked my lists of random ideas, and, of course, dipped into my time line sources. This time I got lucky. For April 3 was not just the date of the speech, it was also the anniversary of the inauguration of the Pony Express. So what, right? Well, what caught my eye was something I had not realized.

I had thought that the Pony Express was a sort of nineteenth-century institution, a long-running (no pun intended) service that was an integral part of opening up the frontier. Hadn't Buffalo Bill been a Pony Express rider? Absolutely. What an icon of growth and expansion, I thought, a great example of the power of speed, for the service cut mail delivery time between the eastern terminus in St. Joseph's, Missouri, and the western end at Sacramento from three weeks or more to just ten days.

Imagine my surprise, then, when I found out that this symbol of the Old West, of brave young men and swift horses, existed for only about eighteen months. A year and a half. What happened? The telegraph, that's what happened. For its time, it was the quintessential disruptive technology. And when the Pacific Telegraph Company completed its line to San Francisco in October 1861, it sent a strong message to the backers of the Pony Express: "You're finished."

Great little story. Fully on topic. And an analogy I, for one, had not seen used before. Plus, it had the advantage of having a very clear visual image built in. Young men on swift horses, racing through the sagebrush, dodging tumbleweed, traversing gulches and gullies, speeding along on their appointed rounds. A host of strong brand attributes captured in two words: Pony Express. Plus the kicker, which I was convinced most people did not know about—in existence for just eighteen months. It was a story that, at first glance, had nothing to do with what my client wanted to say. But in the end, it was a story that made the connection with the audience and raised the talk above the mundane.

Being memorable means exercising your imagination, your creativity. And creativity, like innovation, is not about coming up with something entirely new every time. More often than not, it's about putting well-known things together in a new way.

The Provocation Hook

Most speeches are boring. Agree? Disagree? I don't really care. What I care about is that I got your attention.

Because just as you can lead a horse to water without his taking a drink, you can fill a room with an audience without making them thirst for your words of wisdom. Sometimes you need a more in-your-face approach to catch their ear. And a provocative statement just might fit the bill.

In most cases, the provocative statement will have part of the audience sitting up straight and thinking, "Finally, someone has the intestinal fortitude to tell it like it is." At the same time, another part of the audience will be feeling the hackles rise on the backs of their necks at your outrageous effrontery. "Who does this person think he is? Why I oughta . . ." And the rest of them will at least be asking themselves how in the world you're going to get yourself out of this corner.

Any way you slice it, you've got them hooked . . . a little bit of drama right from the time the curtain goes up. It's like finding a body in the first scene of a whodunit. You don't even have to believe in this provocative statement. The objective is to get attention, not set out your life's philosophy. But it sure helps if your shock-and-awe tactic has some connection with reality. It should represent at least one faction, albeit a radical one, of the issue you want to pursue. And if it's palpably true, but a truth that everyone has been pussyfooting around, well, you've got a winner.

The most compelling example of this that I was involved with was during my time as a staff speechwriter for a giant electric utility. This utility produced electricity for Canada's most populous province from a variety of hydro plants (most notably at Niagara Falls), nuclear reactors, and coal and gas-fired facilities. As a quasi-government-run organization, it was subject to significant levels of oversight, not only from its only shareholder (the Ontario government) but also from a raft of interest groups. In particular, the environmental lobby had had this company in its sights for many years.

In response, the company had repeatedly bragged about its concern for the environment, pointing out how often it had relocated power lines to avoid the only known habitat of some rare tree frog or owl or whatever. At the time as well, the environmentalists had succeeded in getting the government to impose limits on the pollutants the utility could release into the air, mostly from its coal- and gas-fired plants, which spewed hundreds of thousands of tons of noxious residue into the air every year. These limits, it must be said, were pretty liberal, giving the utility plenty of leeway to reduce the mess they were creating, and time to do it.

Then along comes a new chairman with an ear that is more sympathetic to the arguments of the tree huggers and an impatience for change within the large, bloated, and intransigent bureaucracy that characterized the utility at the time. He wanted a new, meaningful pro-environment program within this company. And he wanted people to know it.

Clearly, there would be a full-out public relations assault on the media to let the world know that Ontario Hydro and the environment were *simpatico*. And the campaign would begin with a major speech. Trouble was, as we sifted through the files on what we'd said before, it seemed as if it had all been said before. We'd always said we were on the side of the white hats—or I suppose, in this case, the green hats. What could we say now that would make people think that this time maybe we meant it, that this time, maybe we'd follow through?

Fortuitously, we had just received what on the surface looked like some terrible news. We had just been sent a consultants' study that showed that Ontario Hydro was, at least at the time, the worst corporate polluter in the country. Lucky, eh? From my perspective, it didn't get much better than that, for after the initial hand-wringing, it slowly dawned on us that we had been handed a terrific way to get attention for this important speech.

It took only a brief discussion until the chairman saw the potential here for the company to draw attention to its more aggressive environmental strategy, to clearly mark a change from past platitudes, and for him to place an indelible stamp on the new direction. The opening line? The provocative statement?

"It would be nice for me to be able to stand in front of you today and describe an Ontario Hydro with a spotless record on the environment. But the fact of the matter is, you're looking at the chairman and president of a corporation that is one of Ontario's major sources of pollution." Two short sentences. One in particular starkly stating what everybody suspected but no one had ever admitted, certainly not anyone at the utility.

Of course, that was just a starting point. For after that came his real message: "I'm not proud to say that. But nor am I about to hide from the reality that making electricity does disturb the environment. What I want to do today is leave you with the clear understanding of Hydro's commitment to help make this province a better place to live. To us, that means continuing to supply reliable electricity at low cost while at the same time doing all we can to limit our impact on the ecology."

The *mea culpa* made the commitment credible. And then he spent the next fifteen minutes outlining the course of action and a timetable for changing the utility's relationship with Mother Earth. It was a remarkably courageous thing to do for a man in his position. He had been given his position, and held on to it, at the whim of the provincial government, and we all knew how fickle politicians can be, especially when they see such an obvious scapegoat. He could have been buying the gasoline that the interest groups would now fling onto the fire. All the while recognizing that the utility's track record on pollution predated his tenure by decades.

But none of that happened. In fact, by taking accountability, he co-opted the environmentalists, turning rabid opposition into, if not allies, at least opponents with a wait-and-see attitude toward the utility's new initiatives. In the room, at the time, you could have heard a pin drop after that opening. He had them, not only for the twenty minutes he spoke, but for many weeks afterwards.

Of course, the risks of such candor are great. If you talk a good game, you have to back it up with action. Because someone will always remember the promises you made and keep track of which ones you've kept. You cannot be swept up in the immediate emotional charge you might get from provoking an audience.

You must also take into account your ability to deliver over the longer term on the shock and awe you're inciting. For if your speech is any good, if it is memorable, it *will* be remembered, and you may well be called to account for how you lived up to your rhetoric. If you can walk the talk, you've done immeasurable good for your cause, and for your own brand.

Another way to provoke the crowd is to set up straw men—or women, as the case may be. You paint a picture, lay out an argument, capture in twenty-five words or less the salient thrust of a particular point of view. And then proceed to tear it apart over the next fifteen minutes or so. It's like having a debate over two sides of an issue, only you're the only one doing the talking. How great is that?

Call it myth-busting, if you like, for very often that's exactly the way the script unfolds. In one recent speech with which I was involved, the speaker wanted to present the company's position on the regulatory environment around the telecommunications industry. But he wanted to be more provocative (his word) than the usual lawyerly stuff that the company, in its great gray wisdom, had been wont to put out. So we worked up a scenario in which he would take on—head-on—the three top myths of the industry post–dot-gone meltdown. In so doing, he was giving some prominence to what the competitors were saying, in contrast to many speakers who wouldn't dare mention the opposition. But he was then able to marshal an impressive amount of information—both data-driven and anecdotal—to demolish the opposing claims quicker than Perry Mason in front of a prevaricating witness.

After a brief opening, the speaker got down to business like this: "I suggest we start by dispelling the persistent myths that obscure the realities of our sector. I want to talk about just three of the more general—and more egregious—of them. Myth #1:

The deflation of the dot-com bubble proved that the Internet is just froth. And by implication, the information and communications technology sector is not as important a contributor to economic growth as people once thought. Myth #2: The amount of regulation in the telecommunications sector is decreasing. And Myth #3: Telecommunications is not competitive enough.

These were three provocative statements that formed the outline and architecture of the rest of the speech, enabling the speaker both to discount the position of others and to promote the position of his company, directly and by implication. In fact, he didn't say anything different than company spokespeople had been saying for quite some time. But he said it differently, and that made a big difference, not only in the room, but also later.

Certainly, the audience responded well to his modest in-your-face efforts. But the buzz around the speech also put the speaker on the media map, establishing him more prominently as someone with a clear point of view that he is not afraid to express. That pays dividends almost daily as the speaker is quoted frequently in news reports of the ongoing debate around telecommunications regulation.

Provocation: It's a powerful way to connect. But don't forget to back it up, not only in the speech, but in real action from that day forward.

Connect Through Listening

Remember, the forum for any speech is a confluence of agendas—if not a clash. The organizers have their own objectives, which most often include putting bums in the seats so they can make a little money for their efforts at bringing all these great thinkers together. You as the speaker have your own goals, for your cause and for yourself. But the third partner in this little tri-

angle is the one most people forget. And it's only the most important. The audience.

What is their objective? What do they expect? More important,
what do they want? It's trite to say that communications is a two-
way street. There has to be a sender and a receiver. Trite but true.
But it's easy to forget that the audience has a stake in what is
being said as you worry about being able to get all your messages
out there in a meaningful way.

If you don't connect at least moderately with what your audience expects and wants to hear, all the messaging, all the message massaging in the world, won't make your talk memorable
to them. And there's no way to find out what's important to your
audience without listening to them. There are many ways to do
that.

Most conference organizers have producers that have done at
least some research on what their target market is interested in.
Sometimes, you can get feedback reports from previous years to
see what participants valued and what they didn't. Another way
to open up the feedback loop is to tap into your own grapevine
within and outside of your organization. A simple phone call will
often get you something:

"If you were going to the Widget Summit, what are the top couple of issues you'd expect to be addressed? Do you think the audience would be interested in the Plus-X story, or is it too narrowly
focused?"

Oftentimes, executives will circulate a draft speech to friends,
colleagues, counterparts (even spouses) before they give their
final blessing. That's all good, even the input from the spouse
(most of the time). But why not go one step further and solicit
input from this personal focus group before getting down to putting ink on paper, or rearranging pixels on the screen? Listening
to their ideas up front may keep you out of a few blind canyons of
reasoning, or uncover a rich mother lode that had not even
showed up on your own Geiger counter. And it can't help but

bring you closer to the maelstrom of ideas that is undoubtedly percolating in the minds of your audience.

It's also been a practice of the senior executives with whom I've worked to "suss" out the audience *in situ.* By that I mean they show up early to work the room, glad-handing old buddies and making new contacts. This serves a couple of very important purposes. One, it warms the speaker up, making sure he or she is game-ready before the spotlight narrows to just them. It also establishes a more intimate connection between the person on the platform and those in the peanut gallery. That tends to ease the nervous stomach most speakers feel before they thank the person introducing them.

From a substantive point of view, it enables the speaker to probe a little bit for top-of-mind issues among the guests, and even to unearth a telling anecdote or two that can be thrown in as an ad-lib that, in and of itself, adds to the immediacy and memorability of the content. This is also a chance for the speaker to assess whether their canned material is hitting all the right hot buttons. And they then have even more potential hooks to make the connection with the audience, by referring to a specific listener or an anecdote heard over cocktails.

It's the kind of thing that creates dynamism in your speech, which is, after all, a live event. It reflects great respect for your audience, to hear what some of them have just been talking about referred to by you. It tells them you care about their role in this little drama and connects you with what they care about. And connecting, after all, is what it's all about.

Key Points

- Connect with the audience through story, location, time, or a provocative straw man.

- Draw a tangible word picture, an image that captures the head-line of the speech.

- Use image and metaphor as a key to the theater of the mind . . . and a shorthand link to meaning that creates memories.

Keep the Focus on You

Before you begin to write, there is one more thing you have to consider, for it will color your entire approach to—and interaction with—your audience. In my view, it is the pandemic that killed a million presentations. It is the big fluffy cotton ball that muffles thought. It is the washed-out bridge that separates the speaker from the audience. "It" is slideware.

Probably no other single thing has done so much to degrade the quality of the modern speech while paradoxically fueling the number of speeches that actually get made. Not that long ago, even at the end of the 1980s, many organizations were having to pay outside suppliers $20 to $25 per slide to create the transparencies that the speaker would then drop into a carousel and hope the thing would work—that the carousel would turn, that the slides would properly drop down into the aperture, and up again when asked, that the lens would stay focused, the light stay on, but not so long as to actually burn the slide.

In those days, people took care with their slideware. They minimized its use. Often, because of the production headaches associated with real slides, they would forgo the expense and risk and they would just talk, tightly focused on what they were saying and how the audience was reacting.

Today, it's a different story. Corporations, educators, researchers—all of them collectively churning out trillions of slides to allegedly illustrate what they are saying. Most do it on PowerPoint software, born in 1984 (ominous?) and driven—or built—into the computers of more than 400 million users through the marketing power of Microsoft. "Give me a deck on that" is often the first command out of the boss's mouth. "We've got twenty minutes to speak? Give me twenty or thirty slides and we'll build the story around that."

In some organizations, no one gets up to speak without a laptop full of slides. Business plans and strategies are reduced to bullets on rich blue backgrounds. Got a major speech? What will we put on screen behind the speaker?

No question, PowerPoint and other software in its class make it easy to create slides and edit them and rearrange them virtually up to the time you clear your throat to say "Good morning." It's a great product. But it's the wrong product, most of the time, if your objective is to create a lasting impression.

Don't take my word for it. Edward Tufte is professor emeritus of political science, computer science and statistics, and graphic design at Yale University. His assessment of the rise of what he calls "chartjunk" is withering: "It induced stupidity, turned everyone into bores, wasted time, and degraded the quality and credibility of communication."[1]

And he's not finished yet. Being in thrall to slideware "routinely disrupts, dominates, and trivializes content. Thus, PowerPoint presentations too often resemble a school play—very loud, very slow, and very simple."[2] And yet more: "Presentations largely stand or fall on the quality, relevance, and integrity of the content. If your numbers are boring, then you've got the wrong numbers. If your words or images are not on point, making them dance in color won't make them relevant. Audience boredom is usually a content failure, not a decoration failure."[3]

Amen to all that.

In Tufte's view, much of the trouble with slideware is that it oversimplifies data. Because space on the slide is limited, a speaker can provide only a very high level view, losing nuance and most important context. By their very nature, slide presentations also impose a linear, sequential structure to the talk. Some material lends itself to that, if you are intent on transmitting data and logical steps only. But human experience is anything but linear. And logic will not connect you with the audience.

Tufte's concern about context is probably his most telling point. Because I like to see what other people are doing and saying in their speeches, I often request copies after the fact. I am amazed at the number of times the copy arrives as simply a sheaf of slide printouts, with no notes attached. Most times, those copies are all but useless to me. They are prepared in a shorthand that only those in the room could possibly decipher and then only when the speaker has unlocked the translation keys. So I also have no idea how credible or engaging the speaker was from seeing his or her slides. And the aftermarket value of the presentation is reduced to zero. You can send the slides around to colleagues and customers, but that's unlikely to win friends or influence people.

There are numerous other problems with using slides, some technical, some more fundamental. On the technical side is how much or how little information can actually be carried by the slide. A single slide cannot usefully contain a lot of material. Oh, you can squeeze a lot on, but once you get up above forty words or so, it won't be legible from very far back in the audience. And that's without trying to jam on a couple of graphs, a headline, and a bumper (the little recap at the bottom). So that's less than helpful to the people you're trying to impress. And if you cut the information down to what can easily be visible from great distances, you end up with a huge number of slides, each of which shows a very narrow band of information—like the slices of information in a CAT scan of the brain.

The constant changing of slides reinforces the linearity of the talk and creates a constant diversion as the audience tries to read each one, put it into some context with the prior slides, and listen to you all at the same time. Then there is the problem with the way many people use slides. It is common to see speakers actually read the bullet points to the audience. Frankly, I haven't needed to have anyone read to me for a long, long time. Maybe it's because the print is too small, because they're trying to say too much on each slide, because someone has told them no more than twenty slides. So they spend their time and yours apologizing for the illegibility of each slide. "Don't know if you can read this at the back, but here's what I am getting at." How often do you hear that? And how disrespectful is it of the audience that the speaker couldn't be bothered to make sure those watching could read it?

Another issue is the structure that many slides enforce on speakers. The typical presentation begins with a title slide (boring), then an agenda slide. Only then, on slide 3, does the speaker begin to get to the meat. It's the old conventional structure of tell 'em what you're doing to say, say it, then tell 'em what you said. It shows little or no creativity, beyond that of the visual ingenuity of your graphic designer. And it's boring.

As you click from slide to slide, inserting an updated agenda slide every time you switch to a big new topic area, what you're mostly doing is helping the audience gauge how much longer they have to count their teeth with their tongues until you're finished.

To be fair, the arguments in favor of slides are also many and varied. But to my mind they're not worth the software they're written with.

1. Slides help the audience keep track of where you are in the presentation. First, let me repeat, your audience is not stupid. If your spoken text is sufficiently logical and interesting, they'll be able to follow without the visual bookmarks. If you're doing it right, you'll keep them on the edge of their seats precisely because they *don't* necessarily know where you are in the presentation. But they're willing to listen till you pull all the strings together at the end.

One technique I use in all-words, no-slides speeches is to pepper it with epigrams. Early on, I set up a key phrase. Then at the appropriate points throughout the speech, I'll just throw in that phrase again, to change the pace, to break the flow, to signal a shift to a new concept, or just to bring everybody back to the starting point, to remind them what my thesis is. Thus, in a speech about change where the opening story is about the extinction of the Stephens Island wren, all you have to do to capture the whole concept of adaptability, flexibility, whatever your emphasis might be, is to throw in a couple of references to the unfortunate bird. "Remember the Stephens Island wren." Or "we can't afford to be like the Stephens Island wren." Just two or three times in the course of the speech. Keeps everyone organized, and focused on you and your point.

2. Slides help me keep track of where I am in the presentation. This is the crutch argument, heard a lot from inexperienced speakers. If you need slides to keep you on track, maybe you don't know enough about what you're talking about to be up there in front of the crowd.

3. Slides provide visual flair—they're attractive and look cool. Yes and no. Yes, in that designers can make some pretty attractive-looking visual aids. The software is so good that almost anyone, in fact, can make a pretty picture. But you shouldn't invest too much in that visual appeal. Remember, this is an audience that later that night, or on the weekend, will drop $15 to watch *Matrix IV* or *Lord of the Rings Part VIII* or *Helen of Troy*, complete with fleets of computer-generated Greek warships spread across the Aegean Sea. The point? No matter how pretty your pictures, no matter how you fly in your bullet points, they are not going to be visually impressive to people who have seen aliens blow up the White House. No, your slides may be pretty, but they won't be a substitute for substance, for ideas.

4. Slides are good because a picture is worth a thousand (or ten thousand) words. Again, yes and no. In our postliterate age, many people respond most readily to visual images. But the canned stock photography shots that grace most slides look exactly like what they are: canned stock shots that are about as exciting as the photos in a Sears catalogue. And the graphs that are another stock in trade are sterile depictions of numerical ratios. They are not totally useless, but nor are they something on which you want to hang your entire connection with the audience.

What's more, the vast majority of slides today—at a guess, more than 90 percent—don't have any images on them. They are an endless barrage of bullet points, short, sharp, insistent, and about as subtle as a poke in the eye. Slides are a visual medium, but people treat it as if it were a fourth-grade blackboard—albeit with colored chalk. So this particular argument fails, not so much on its merit, but in practice.

By now you may think I believe slides should never be used. Of course not. Like anything else, they have their uses. It's just that they should be used sparingly and only in specific applications. For instance, slides can be a very useful tool in helping to tell the financial story of a company to the investment community. For one thing, it's what the audience expects. And when you're talking to investors, surprise is not a good thing. For another, both speaker and spoken to are generally talking the same language. They know the various shorthand names for earnings, and they like to see the trends that can be plotted on a graph.

But the slide is still a tool. It doesn't tell the story in and of itself. It only illustrates, enables a sort of code to be transmitted between speaker and listener. So if you insist on using a slide, remember what you're using it for—to illustrate your point. And I mean illustrate literally. If you can't turn what you're saying into a picture, don't put it on a slide. A photo or a chart, and a headline —that's about all you should ever need.

Given my misgivings about slideware, my advice to clients is always to at least consider delivering a speech without slides. I get religious about it when it's a CEO involved in a keynote speech, or anything involving a meal. I have too many memories, I suppose, of after-lunch slide presentations in school, when the lights would dim, the steady click of the carousel would create a nice, drowsy rhythm, and learning . . . well, who's going to know if I just rest my eyes?

More critical, however, is this: I don't think any CEO or senior executive should set him- or herself up to be a slide jockey, the speechmaking equivalent of the airhead vid-jocks who spend their lives filling empty airtime between videos on MTV. The people in the audience came to see you, to hear you. Not to watch you push a button. Not to be distracted by pictures. The slides—a cold medium—essentially cut off the warm, human connection you as a person, as a brand, can make with your audience. You're not there to show off how good your graphic artist is. You're there to show off your wit, your wisdom, your erudition. And that's what the audience wants too.

So think twice —no, think many times—before agreeing to hide your incandescence behind the light of the projector lamp.

A Modest Prop-osal

While we're on the subject of audiovisual aids, let me comment briefly on two more popular and almost always lame techniques common in speechmaking.

One of the elements theater directors use to make the experience more real, more entertaining, is props. Swords, giant red flags waving in the background of miserable revolutionary youths—you know what I mean. It's an element many speakers also love to use. But almost invariably I ask myself why.

It's particularly common in the high-tech industry, where speakers will be oh so proud to show off their latest handheld supercomputer or color screen, full video phone. So at one point in the speech, they pull this marvelous device out of their pocket and hold it up. Question is, who can see it beyond the first two rows? And even the people up front can't really tell what it does, not when they're twenty feet away from a device designed to be viewed at no more than arm's length.

Simple solution, say the a/v wizards. We'll get a video camera and project a close-up of the device in the speaker's hand, as he or she makes it work. Ok, so now everyone can see it. But to my mind, the distraction this causes is more pain than it's worth. First, the attention of the audience is diverted away from the speaker and what he or she is saying. Then the camera person creates a bit of a fuss just getting into position. But most important, the Gee Whiz! factor of these devices—if there is one—comes to light only when you actually hold one in your hand, not when you essentially watch a movie about someone watching a news clip on a two-inch screen.

I've also often seen purveyors of software try a similar thing with a laptop screen projected onto large screens so everyone can see the product in action. Sorry. Watching some pixels re-arrange themselves on a screen in a prebaked demo is not my idea of stimulating entertainment. Because the product is not about pixels moving around on the screen, I presume. It's about what that enables the user to do—save time, find inefficiencies, cook the books, whatever. And no demonstration will show that. Better to find a customer who will say it.

I have the same major reservations about inserting a video into a speech. Executives often want to use the latest glossy promo video, thinking that it somehow adds excitement and dynamism to their presentation. Unlikely. Mostly, it breaks the rhythm of the talk, snaps any connection the speaker has made with the audience to that point, and demonstrates the skill—or lack thereof—of whatever supplier made the video. Oh yes, it does give the speaker a chance to catch his or her breath and have a drink of water.

Video is a momentum killer. No matter how flashy the photography. No matter how loud or upbeat the music. It's a different medium than the live theater the speaker is starring in at the moment. It not only requires the audience to switch gears, it can also invite them to switch off, given that most corporate videos are cut from exactly the same cloth.

Sometimes, I repeat, sometimes a video can work for an internal audience, one that is predisposed to be proud of the company. But almost never have I seen one work for an external crowd. If you insist on using a video, take great care you have the appropriate venue. And consider very seriously using it before you get started—and nowhere else. Use it as a prelude, while you're walking up. At least then it won't interrupt your rhythm, your flow, or the rapport that you—you, the real, live, flesh-and-blood person—work so hard to establish with the audience.

Key Points

- Slides do not enhance your personal brand.

- Slides reduce your ability to repackage the presentation for after-market distribution.

- Slides and videos distract attention from your words and ideas.

- Videos and demonstrations break the logical flow, dissipate drama and energy.

- Use sparingly if at all.

Notes

1. Edward Tufte, "PowerPoint Is Evil: Power Corrupts. Power-Point Corrupts Absolutely," *Wired.com*, issue 11.09, Condé Naste Publications (September 2003).
2. Ibid.
3. Ibid.

As You Write

Reading maketh a full man, conference a ready man and writing an exact man.

—FRANCIS BACON

10

Getting Down to It

All right. You've put it off long enough. But now it's time to actually write something. You've done the research. You know what the audience is looking for and what you're prepared to say. You know your main points and have reams of backup material to bolster your prescient trend-spotting and high-flying conclusions. Now you must answer the how question. How do you put it all into a twenty-minute capsule that (1) you can deliver with some conviction and (2) the audience will remember not just through the next coffee break but in the weeks and months ahead.

Remember one word: *simplicity*. This does not mean writing for simpletons. It does not mean dumbing down so the thirtieth percentile and below of the audience can understand what you're saying. Simplicity means clarity of thought and expression. Directness. Candor. It means using images, metaphors, examples, whatever other techniques are in your bag to simplify sometimes complex ideas, to give the ethereal some tangible heft.

Simplicity means respecting the audience, both their intelligence and the task you're expecting them to carry out—that is, to sit still for twenty minutes to listen to your ideas. It is the words you decide to use that will either make the connection you need with your listeners . . . or not. The force of your personality, your stage presence, your position in whatever hierarchy you're part of—all these play important roles in making your appearance memorable. But without the words, all else is simply empty echoes.

Small Words. Big Ideas.

The days of high-flown oratory are gone. Better to stick to plain words, simply spoken. Point made. Lasting impression.

Here's a little experiment that can be eye—and ear—opening. Tape-record the next conference call or meeting you attend at which memos will be issued afterwards to recap the proceedings. Then compare what people said in the meeting with what the memo says. My bet is that there will be a huge difference. Not in substance; the memo may well capture accurately the discussion and next steps. The difference will be in style. Most people write in a different style from how they talk. We talk normally, using plain old everyday English. But something happens when we sit down at a keyboard to write. It's as if a little devil inside our head compels us to gussy up the language for fear of being seen as somehow not advanced enough to do the job. So *use* becomes *utilize. Speed* becomes *velocity. Layoffs* become *workforce adjustments. Fired* becomes *leaving the company to pursue other opportunities.*

Some of that toning up is social convention, meant to soften the unpalatable truth. It's nice to hope that old Frank actually might have other opportunities to pursue, although knowing old Frank, we can't imagine who in his right mind would offer him one. But a lot of word upscaling is showing off. Writing things down gives us a chance to think a bit—unlike talking—so that we can search our brains and our thesauruses for really good words that show how bright—make that erudite—we are. We all do it to some extent. "Why use a nickel word when I know a 25-cent word with many syllables? That'll impress 'em that I'm educated and articulate."

Trouble is, sometimes the big word isn't quite right. A thesaurus can be a dangerous thing, with many a nuance lost between the resource and the finished product. *Speed* and *velocity*, for instance, are not synonyms, for *velocity* has within its meaning both speed and direction. It's a perfectly good word, but it ain't simply speed. *Presently*, for another example, doesn't mean now; it means in a little while. More important, when people try to get fancy in their choice of words, they invariably make it tougher for whoever is on the receiving end to figure out exactly what is being communicated. In certain cases, that may well be the objective of the writer who is tasked with getting out something about which he is none too sure. But most times, it is a misplaced sense of gravitas: "If the President is going to read this, it had better be at a level significantly above my usual watercooler chitchat."

The question is, why? Why camouflage ambiguity in big words? Why make it tougher for the recipient to understand what actually went on at the meeting, what decisions were made, what steps have yet to be trod? So when people approach the writing of a speech, they tend to see it as a make-or-break experience. "This is a big deal, keynote talk to the annual meeting of America's Widget Makers. I have to be good. No, I have to be scintillating, brilliant, luminous, exhilarating." They feel it's incumbent upon them to elucidate, illuminate, excoriate.

Don't know about you, but I don't think I've ever used any of those words in a real, live conversation with normal people. So why would I expect to use them in a real, live speech to normal people? After all, it's still a conversation, albeit a little bit one-sided. And you don't have to believe me. Bill Clinton was—and probably still is—one of the most effective speakers of our times.

He had to be, not just to get elected twice but also to cling to office and continue to be held in high esteem by a significant portion of the population. In the White House, he used to tell his speech-writers that, no matter the audience, no matter the weight of the subject matter, he wanted them to imagine that he was at home, talking to family and friends in his living room.

Clinton would routinely go through the drafts they sent up the chain with a fine-tooth editing pen, stroking out any phrase that smacked of even the least bit of rhetorical flourish. He insisted on the use of simple, concrete words. When one syllable would do the work of some multisyllabic mouthful, he chose it. And for good reason. For not only are big, complex words harder to say, they are also harder to listen to. As well, string enough of them together, and they establish a sleep-inducing rhythm of their own.

The same goes for the length of your sentences. Long sentences with a lot of subordinate phrases and clauses may be all right in written work. After all, a complex idea often needs to be surrounded with context and caveats and can be tough to express in a short declarative sentence. But capturing that nuance in a work to be delivered orally and received aurally, well, that must be managed differently.

Try it out yourself. Take a sentence from a report you've written that spreads out over 40 or 50 words. Read it out loud. Unless you're a pearl diver, you'll likely have to take a breath somewhere in the middle. That break may be just enough to throw your audience off course, especially if you're in the middle of a complex, closely reasoned argument. Better to divide the sentence into two or more breath-sized segments. Even if they don't add up to grammatically correct full sentences. Like this.

That is not to say your speech should be an endless succession of short, pithy sentences with the odd fragment thrown in to break up a difficult idea. As in anything, variety is the spice. The staccato effect of punchy sentences can get as annoying as the soft somnolence of a string of long, involved statements. But on balance, shorter is better, in words and sentences.

Take this excerpt from a speech by Lee Iacocca as an example:

> Take cars. Japan exports more than half the cars it builds. And half of them come to the United States. Because their competition is so intense, Japanese car companies are just breaking even in their home market. And they barely do the same with their exports to Europe and the rest of the world. The only place that the Japanese car industry makes any real profit is here in America.[1]

One paragraph. Six sentences. The average length of sentence is eleven and two-thirds words. The shortest sentence is two words; the longest one, seventeen. The longest word is four syllables (*America*, *competition*—both of which are common, easily understood, and easy to say). He varies the pace, moving from very short to longer as he moves more assuredly to his punch line. The point is clear and forcefully made. It's easy to say and to hear, delivered in plain language. And it's quite clear: Plain does not mean dull. It means direct and precise, using exactly the right word, leaving no room for misunderstanding or misperceptions.

It's not as if your audience can go back over what you've just said to see if they heard you right. In the moment, they have to be able to get it. Otherwise you risk losing them and muffling the impact of your argument. So plain language means never wasting words, or even syllables, when perfectly acceptable alternatives are available from the vocabulary you use in everyday speech in the car pool or around the dinner table. And that's the key: The days of overwrought oratory are behind us.

We live in a postliterate age. It used to be that one could invoke the powers of Thor, the horrors of the Stygian stables, or Helenic beauty, and audiences would nod sagely. But now we must trim our verbal sails. Such allusions are likely to be met with uncomprehending stares. Here's Iacocca again, same speech:

> Of all the people in history, Ben Franklin is the man I'd most like to meet. I'd like to have a drink with him. (I'd have a scotch and he'd have his glass of port.) He'd probably start by saying, 'Iacocca. That's a hell of a name. I never heard a name like that before!' And I'd tell him all about the big waves of immigrants that came over. (I'd probably talk a lot about that because since I got involved with the Statue of Liberty and Ellis Island project, I've become something of an expert.)[2]

Well, the auto magnate was never known for his modesty. But he was known for his straight talk. No question, there are rhetorical tricks at work here, but they are more subtle than the old style flights of fancy and verbosity. In this excerpt, he clearly takes the audience into his confidence, as it were, in the parenthetical phrases. We become more intimate friends, knowing that he tipples the nectar of the peat bogs, that he's proud of his immigrant heritage, and that he's acting on that pride with volunteer work.

It's all done in language that is straightforward and plain, even slightly profane—the way one might talk in the elevator on the way to the lunch room. Not "endless waves of immigrants." Not mountainous waves. Not even huge waves. Just "big waves." No pretentiousness here.

Grammatical purists and writing stylists may blanch to see this style praised. Sentence fragments galore. The use of "hell" in a formal talk. "Talk a lot"? Why not some more elevated word, such as *expound* or *elaborate*? But that is not the man, nor is it the point. The words you use, and the way you put them together in sentences, must reflect the way you normally talk and, just as important, the way the audience normally listens.

That's the starting point. But let me add a few more specific guidelines as you put finger to keyboard. None of these is a hard-and-fast rule. For one thing, that's because no one follows every hard-and-fast rule when talking to friends. For another, the English language is a dynamic, living thing, evolving with great rapidity, influenced by our ever-more global and diverse culture.

The use of pronouns is a case in point. Technically, singular pronouns such as *none* and *no one* take a singular verb and should be followed by a singular pronoun. For example, "No one *is* arriving soon enough to pick up *his* ticket for the performance." Technically correct but awkward in the extreme, especially when one has a lot of references like that in proximity. In fact, normal conversational usage is to say, "No one is arriving soon enough to pick up *their* ticket." Everyone who hears or reads that knows what is meant. No harm, no foul. And the construction is less ungainly than the technically correct one. Even arbiters of usage are beginning to accept this as reasonable, just as they are beginning to soften on the practice of using a preposition to end a sentence with. Plain talk just naturally flows that way. And in the end, what's wrong with that? Nothing.

So certainly, hard-and-fast rules of written English are softening when it comes to spoken English. As well, every rule has its exception. For the most part, though, you can help make your speech more memorable if you keep these in mind:

The Passive Voice Is Not to Be Used

Nothing kills the momentum of the written or spoken word faster than the passive voice. It camouflages accountability. It is the domain of the nameless, faceless, brand-less bureaucrat. For instance, "We met all day and all night. We talked and argued, fought and made up. *It was decided* that the compensation package should be increased by an amount equal to the cost of living for each of the next five years. *It was also felt* that the negotiating team had succeeded in fulfilling its mandate."

The first two sentences are in the active voice, identifying who is involved and what they did. After that, though, it's all downhill. There's a switch to passive voice, so insidious you hardly even notice it. But all of a sudden, we're not quite as sure who is doing what. Who decided? Who felt? The ambiguous *It* becomes the subject. And who *It* is, not even Abbott and Costello know.

Of course, by using the passive voice, people avoid taking responsibility for actions or feelings. Would you say this to your teenager? "It is felt that one shouldn't stay out past one's curfew." Of course not. More likely, you'd say something like this: "I want you home by midnight, or else." You're the one in charge, not some nebulous committee. You're setting the limits, so you make that clear.

Why would you do any different in a speech? "The import levy was deemed inadequate to protect the domestic industry." Ugh. Why not: "I think the tariff is too low!" Or if that's too bold: "The evidence clearly demonstrates that the tariff is too low.'

It's clear. It's unambiguous. And most important, the speaker takes responsibility for his or her opinion.

Avoid Clichés Like the Plague

I admit being of two minds when it comes to clichés. On the one hand, the reason phrases become trite and overused is that they were, at least initially, clever, and they perfectly capture the sentiment people want to express. In that context, they can cut to the chase by providing a sort of verbal shorthand for the listener. On the other hand, of course, clichés induce everything from boredom to shudders of revulsion.

People who pepper their remarks with clichés, consciously or not, frequently demonstrate nothing more than their grasp of the obvious and their apparent lack of creative, original thought. And if the language you use is filled with trite phrases, people may just assume your ideas are similarly unoriginal, noncreative, and decidedly not memorable.

Nothing Memorable in Buzzwords

Buzzwords are related to clichés. They may even be the same thing, although buzzwords tend to flame out much more quickly, seeming to go from "hot button" to "so last century" in the time it takes Roger Clemens to unretire. Their limited shelf life tends to date your speech quickly, reducing your ability to amortize the investment over a long time.

Sometimes these phrases seem to come out of thin air, or at least from some clever T-shirt entrepreneur. "Been there, done that." Often, they're the catchphrase popularized by someone in the relentless eye of the news media or on a hit television series. "Shock and awe" and "embedded" come to mind for the Iraq war generation. In simpler, Nixonian times, it was "at this point in time." Thanks, Bart Simpson, for "Don't have a cow, man." And the Fonz: "Aaaaiiiyyyyyyy!" I love that every time I hear it . . . NOT (thanks, *Friends*).

When I was in the newspaper business, our managing editor sent down a thundering edict that we were to stop referring to our hometown as "this lakeside city." He also banned the word *lady* in all but the official titles of British aristocrats, on the grounds that a female was a woman until she had proven herself to be a Lady. The other big word under the ban was *spectacular*. It seemed that every two-alarm fire, every five-car freeway pileup was branded "spectacular" by reporters and editors alike. It had become our lazy buzzword for anything that burst into flame. "The only time we will allow the use of the word *spectacular* is in our coverage of the second coming of Christ," I recall the editor's memo reading. "And even then, use it sparingly."

But business types have their own wall of shame when it comes to buzzwords and phrases: *going forward, drill down, bottom line, cutting edge, downsizing, heads up, input,* and probably the granddaddy of them all, *paradigm.* There are more, many more. In fact, Lake Superior State University runs an annual contest to find buzzwords that are so obnoxious they ought to be banned from use by anyone. Although I can't agree with all their picks—*liberal* seems to me a reasonable word, as does *alcoholic*—it's worth checking out what a ton of other people say they don't want to hear. And then avoiding the phrases in your speech, for the chances are good, someone in the audience is adding to his or her list for submission to LSSU. To see the list, visit *http://www .lssu.edu/banished/complete_list.php.*

Adjective Pileups Obscure Meaning

Maybe it's a symptom of the convergent world. Maybe it's simply the time of man. But why is it that so many people seek to cram so many adjectives in front of a single noun? Here's an example of adjective pileup:

> This solution is an integrated financial analytic application suite that provides organizations with the ability to streamline . . .

Here we have four descriptors of the noun *suite*, piled up like a logjam in the midst of a sentence. It's simply too much information to wade through before you get to the point of the phrase—the noun itself. To say nothing of the fact that each adjective is a mouthful in and of itself, and an abstraction that carries with it a whole other level of complexity.

Here's another sample:

> "Recent customer-initiated performance proof of concept tests have proven . . ."

What? I have read that a dozen times and I still am unsure what the tests are. "Performance proof of concept" is absolute gibberish. Again, the speaker is trying to convey too much at one time.

When you find yourself writing a similar string of adjectives, stop and ask how critical it is to include all those descriptors. Most of them you could eliminate with no harm done. Remember, this is an oral presentation. The audience has to be able to follow your flow. And you can't keep them guessing as to when the string of adjectives will end and the noun will pop up, allegedly making it all clear. One or at most two adjectives is all you should expect your audience to be able to handle. Anything more calls for a rewrite—or the delete button.

Jettison the Jargon

The use of jargon is an area where you have to apply some judgment. Like a good cliché, a properly used piece of jargon can cut through a lot of verbiage, enabling you to get to the point quickly and directly. That is, as long as everyone in the audience has a reasonable chance of knowing what the jargon means.

Jargon includes acronyms, short neo-words formed out of the first letters of a bunch of other words: NATO, for instance, for the North Atlantic Treaty Organization, or IBM, which used to stand for International Business Machines but now just stands for IBM. Pretty recognizable and probably don't need to be spelled out. They and other bits of common jargon are part of the vernacular and should be within the knowledge base of most reasonably well educated people. Radar, for instance, is one that has actually entered the language, and most people think it's a word unto itself (perhaps not realizing that it is actually short for "radio detecting and ranging").

But there is a risk to using jargon. On the one hand, it can establish a higher level of intimacy with members of the audience who get the term's meaning without explanation. It identifies them as members of a club. But if jargon includes those in the know, it also tends to be exclusionary for those who aren't. It sets up you and those who understand you as clearly separate from—and slightly above—the hoi polloi who are not in on the big secret.

You can stand up in front of an audience full of people from the telecommunications industry and be pretty sure they'll know what VoIP and DSL and DTH mean. But don't try it in a roomful of bankers. It will serve only to distance them from you. And making solid, memorable connections over a long distance is not that simple, no matter what the phone company says.

Make It Concrete

Abstractions have their place—probably in the Guggenheim Museum, but not in a speech. All right. One can talk about abstractions such as freedom and liberty and justice. But to make all those ideals real for your audience, try to find concrete words, anecdotes, and images that your audience can latch onto.

Even some factual content needs to be humanized to make it more digestible and at the same time memorable. Numbers, for instance, as in statistics, are great favorites of people who want to have a lot of "substance" in their pronouncements. But statistics are like neon—they are inert. Unless you put a charge into them, they tend to lie there, leaving no visible trace of ever having been raised in conversation. That's because so few of us can visualize big numbers. What's a billion, after all? So it's customary to try to translate a figure into something tangible. That's why you see statements like this: "If you went to the bank and took out in one dollar bills all the money investors lost in the Enron fiasco, and laid them all end to end, you would have a line that would stretch from downtown Houston to the moon and back three times . . ." or whatever. Right idea, but the execution leaves something to be desired. Trouble is, people can't get their heads around how far it is to the moon either, because 250,000 miles is beyond their scope of experience too. So use concrete comparisons that people can actually handle. For instance, every year on Earth, about 150 million babies are born, give or take. Now, that happens to be equivalent to the population of Turkey and Egypt combined. But how helpful is that if you've never been to Turkey or Egypt? What is likely to be more impactful is to break the number down to something they understand. For instance, by dividing 150 million by 365, then by 24 and then by 60, you arrive at the fact that every second of every day, just under five new babies are born on earth. That, people can understand.

And that, of course, gets me thinking that therefore there must be at least 4.75 babies conceived every second. From there, it was a short leap to postulate that at any given moment, at least 4.75 couples are having sex somewhere in the world; which then gets me thinking about how low that number probably is, given the number of times the act of love does not lead to a pregnancy, and so on and so on and so on. Not necessarily a fruitful line of inquiry, so to speak. But not an unpleasant thought . . .

But enough of that. The point is simple: Avoid abstract words and numbers. Be as concrete as you can. Make your numbers mean something by connecting them with the normal life experience of the audience.

Don't Get Lost in Translation

Concrete language is absolutely essential when your audience has a significant representation of people who speak a different language than you do. This is true whether they're following along with you on their own or if there is simultaneous translation. Many idiomatic phrases that occur to an English speaker naturally, and would cause an English listener no problem, will be undecipherable to someone who speaks a different language. And translators can have great difficulty finding an equivalent local idiom to convey the same concept, especially if they're not fully briefed in advance. For example: "A revolving pebble does not assemble an emaciated supermodel." Translation: a rolling stone gathers no moss. The point is, at best, obscured.

Humor, in particular, doesn't travel well, as so often it is dependent on the cultural norms it lampoons, norms that differ significantly even among neighbors. Even among Anglophones themselves, there are significant differences in language that you must be careful about. For instance, the word *homely* to a North American generally means physically unattractive, ugly—maybe "great personality" to a kind and imaginative friend. In short, it's no compliment. But say "homely" to a Brit, and he or she will conjure up visions of a warm and cozy hearth with grandma's apple pie cooling on the windowsill.

So when preparing for an international audience, leave the thesaurus, the joke book, and the Big Book of Rhetorical Ruffles and Flourishes on the shelf. Straight talk is the order of the day. Or rather, it's necessary . . . and polite . . . to speak plainly.

He Said, She Said, I Say

They say you can find a statistic to defend almost any point of view on any subject you care to choose. They also say you can find a quotation from the Bible for pretty much any point of view. And Shakespeare's oeuvre, well, it's just chockablock with good stuff on all sorts of human activity. Beyond that, there are literally thousands of people whose words have somehow become immortalized as part of our cultural heritage. And the list is growing as media become more pervasive . . . and arguably more persuasive. "Out, damned spot." It's hard to tell if that's a classical quotation or the slogan for a new laundry detergent.

Some people have said things just so well that it seems pointless to try to say it better. Why not just copy it, with appropriate recognition, of course? I have heard other speechwriters and coaches say, literally, that quotations are the lifeblood of a speech. If that is true, then the substance of the speech is thin broth, indeed. Who doesn't have an old *Bartlett's* kicking around? Who can't type "quotations" into a search engine and then run amok? How often have you heard speakers go to the well? "As Henry Kissinger once said, . . ." or "In the words of Arnold Schwarzenegger, before he was governor. . . ." It's one of the most commonly used tricks in a speaker's bag.

And that's one of the things that's wrong with it. It's common.

It's expected. Ordinary. Normal. Forgettable. Anyone can do it, and usually does. And that's not what we're going for here, is it?

A second drawback to using quotations is credibility. Most of the quotations you'll find in a *Bartlett's* or other source come from people you've never heard of. I like this line: " Guarantees . . . are not worth the paper they are written on." But who the heck is Johann Bernhard, Graf von Rechberg, the author of that phrase? Or Bryan Cornwall (also apparently known as Bryan Waller Procter). Or any of hundreds of other people cited in this and dozens of other quotation resources. And if you don't know who you're quoting or what the person stood for, how useful is the citation?

The third and most important thing wrong with using quotations is that you're ceding the field to someone else. "Wow! If Gandhi agrees with me, I must be right." Trouble is, quoting Gandhi (or anyone else) doesn't show that the person agrees with you. It shows that you agree with the person. And how does "me-too" advance your brand? You're saying to the audience, "Here, remember what this great person said about that? Well, same goes for me. What he said. Ditto."

It does nothing for your brand other than demonstrate that you have either a great memory for what other people have said or some facility for researching a quotation. Neither of which puts you in a strong position vis à vis anyone else who may be on the platform that day. But my objection goes a bit deeper than that. I once worked with a very senior executive (i.e., president of a major company) on his core presentation. This was a series of slides (ugh) that he would use over the course of a year for talks to internal audiences. One or two slides would be modified, deleted, or added to customize the presentation for the particular audience, but most of the content was pretty much static.

One of the themes for this gentleman this particular year was leadership. His objective was to enlist the middle managers he generally addressed to become better "leaders" as opposed to tacticians and managers. Now if you've ever searched for quotations, you know the number of people quoted on leadership is off the charts. And there are some pretty big names there, from people who have actually done it, like Napoleon Bonaparte, to others who have made very successful careers out of studying it, like Peter Drucker.

This executive had once been at an event where Colin Powell gave a speech on leadership. Between that and a general impression of the man, the executive had a sense that Powell was the ultimate expert on the subject. For his presentation, he wanted one slide on leadership as the wrap-up. And on the slide he wanted two or three quotations from Powell on what it meant to be a leader. He felt it would lend gravitas to what he had to say, given that it was coming out of the mouth of one of the leading figures of the western world. Plus, there was no shortage of good material there. Powell has often written and spoken about leadership and has a very succinct and punchy summation of his beliefs, available with just a few keystrokes inside any good search engine. (As a matter of fact, I particularly like Powell's line to the effect that being a leader means being willing to piss some people off.)

But it struck me as odd, in an ironic sort of way, that this senior executive, himself supposed to be a leader of men and women, would resort to parroting the words of someone else. Shouldn't a leader, I said (although not too loudly) actually define leadership in his or her own terms? Does it not lose a bit in the translation, being once removed from the source? Of course not, I was told. Who in the world is a more respected leader than Colin Powell? Not too many people, I said. But I thought: That's the wrong question. He's respected for what *he's* done and how *he* defines what he's done. That's how you have to become a leader: set down your own beliefs, then act on them—with an emphasis on "own."

From my perspective, this executive did not own his leadership rhetoric. He had willingly stepped aside to let a stranger speak for him. That's why my counsel is to use quotations sparingly, if at all. And the higher you go in the hierarchy, the less you should use them. The CEO should be creating his own quotations, not echoing someone else. Own the idea through the words you choose. There are hundreds of thousands of words out there and an infinite number of ways to put them together. Find your own way to say what you need to say.

Quotations Do Have Their Uses

That is not to say that quotations aren't useful. Along with my "Good Stuff" files, I have folders and well-thumbed books full of quotations. Plus I have numerous Web sites bookmarked to let me get at the world of *bon mots*. That's partly because I enjoy reading these beautifully crafted bits of eloquence just for their own sake. But also—and more germane to our purpose here—I find quotations great *thought starters*, pointing my mind in directions it may not have been headed.

So let your eye wander almost aimlessly over the pages, alighting where it will. Open up the imagination. Oil the creative crankshaft. And while they may never end up in a speech you write, the quotations that catch your attention often serve as the catalyst for the idea that makes a speech memorable.

As always, all this is not to say that you should never use quotations. Sometimes they are a very serviceable solution. But if you feel you must, at least attempt to use them in an unconventional, unforgettable way. Work to surprise your audience, not bore them.

For example, one assignment I had was to prepare some remarks for a CEO to deliver to a group of high-achieving salespeople at their annual get-together. These were the cream of the company's revenue generators, enjoying a week at a fancy resort in the Caribbean as compensation for their over-the-top achievements. And while the week was mostly fun, the CEO wanted to go to pat them on the back and light a fire under them for next year.

The talk was at breakfast after the gala awards evening. So it had to be light to compensate for the hungover crowd—and short. But changes were coming in the company, and the CEO had to make a couple of serious business-related points as well. So we sat down to mull over how to accomplish this.

Somehow, I don't remember how, our conversation wandered around to baseball and then to Yogi Berra. Now Yogi must be right up there with Mark Twain and Winston Churchill for "most quoted human being." His whole postbaseball career has been built largely on his endearing ability to mangle the English language. If his name alone weren't enough to bring comic relief, then one of his malapropisms is sure to bring a chuckle. Problem is, it's most often a chuckle of recognition these days. It's not an "Aha!" moment—more of a nostalgic nod of the head to an era that has passed.

The boss and I started to trade one-liners back and forth. "Boy, it gets late early these days." "Nobody goes there anymore; it's too crowded." You know the stuff. After a bit of silence when we ran out of material, the executive said to me, "What if we built the speech around a Yogi quotation?"

Not great, I said, for all those reasons above. Yogi's kind of passé. Too many people use him.

"All right," said the boss. "How about we use 'em all?"

"Touch 'em all?"

"No, use them all. Take about six quotations or more and build a section of the speech around each one of them. "The Gospel of Sales According to Yogi Berra."

And that's what we did. We took half a dozen quotations, one to cover each of the key points the executive wanted to make. And we created a short, funny speech. The feedback was terrific. Seems the audience—despite their pounding heads and parched lips—stayed right with the speaker. Because they knew Yogi's material so well, they actually started to anticipate which quotation would be thrown out there next. And they were keen to see how we'd relate the old chestnuts about a different world to their own high-pressure, high-performance environment.

So there are ways to get away with using quotations. But they're not plentiful. Better to work a bit harder to say it in your own words. Your message will come across as more authentic for sure. And after all, where are the quotes for the next edition of Bartlett's going to come from if we don't try to create them ourselves?

Title Issues

The fax message or phone call will generally come in about 24 hours after you've agreed to share your wisdom with a roomful of strangers in Hoboken. "Can you give us the title of your speech and a synopsis by tomorrow? Our brochure is going to the printer, and we want to make sure to market your speech the right way as soon as possible. Won't take you five minutes."

Okay, so this person has a job to do, and you want to cooperate. After all, you have agreed to the appearance. But you know that a title is a first impression, and in most cases it will leave the most important, most indelible mark on your audience-in-waiting. So you want it to be just right, like a slogan for one of your advertisements. Or like the headline that makes you stop to read about beet futures in China, even though you have no interest in beet futures in China.

Trouble is, you haven't really thought too much about what you'll say, let alone had time to come up with something as clever as a slogan or a headline. And that's no small task. Slapping a title on a piece of work is, in fact, one of the toughest things to do right. Truth be told, it's best done after everything else is written— after you know the beginning, middle, and end of the presentation, after you know your theme and after you've chosen your key right-brain connection with the audience.

It wasn't till after he'd finished *The Great Gatsby,* for instance, that F. Scott Fitzgerald came up with the final title of the American masterpiece. Until then, he'd been working with another title: *Trimalchio in West Egg.* Perhaps it's just 20/20 hindsight, but somehow that doesn't sound like a classic.

In practical terms as well, the normal speech goes through many changes between the time the invitation is accepted and you step up to the microphone. Oftentimes, the just-right title emerges from the research you do for the speech, a happy turn of phrase buried in a mountain of data. Other times, it pops fully formed from your creative mind, occasionally in the middle of the night. And it is never too late to change. In one case, a speaker went to bed the night before a speech with the final version, including title, at the print shop to be copied. When he woke up, he'd hit on a better title sometime during the night. The print shop got some more business, and the speech had the right title. So try to resist being tied to a title too far in advance of your research and writing. Keep your options open.

There's another, more substantive reason for not committing to a title until you absolutely, positively have to: in the long lead time for most speeches, the approach, the topic, even the thesis can change radically several times before the delivery is finalized. A title submitted early in the process to meet some event marketing deadline can be made obsolete as you—and any advisers you may have—dig into what it is you actually want to say.

That's why you should resist organizers' constant desire to pin you into a titular corner before you have thought through the substance of the talk. The organizers do have a job to do, and you should understand that it helps your brand to have your speech properly marketed. But that is less important than the impression made during the speech and in its aftermarketing. Remember: They want you, they need you, and you have some considerable clout in the way you are presented through them.

All of which is to say, when you're pushed into a corner to get a title to the event organizers, stay general to the point of ambiguity so that you can move in any direction as the speech itself evolves. Like this:

> "The [*insert appropriate word here*] Industry: A New Perspective."

> "The Future in Balance: Evolving a New Reality."

You know what I mean: The title says everything and nothing at the same time.

Language Bugaboos

Most writers have their own personal prohibition list—words or phrases that should never be used or, at the very least, great care should be taken when using them. Here are some errors that drive me to the delete button when I'm writing and set my teeth on edge when I hear someone else use them. Chances are, these are on other people's lists, too. In their own way, they signal carelessness and lack of precision—two attributes you never want associated with your personal brand.

- *1 AM in the morning.* Let's not repeat ourselves—AM means "morning."

- *Admit to.* You almost never need the *to*.

- *All intents and purposes.* Overused. Kill on sight. And it is certainly not "all intensive purposes."

- *Any time.* Always two words, no matter what ad copywriters think.

- *At the end of the day (when all is said and done).* Many people, too many people, have fallen in love with this phrase with an intensity that rivals a teenager's obsession with the word *like*. It's a verbal tic, a cliché, and it's almost always unnecessary.

- *Basically.* Almost always superfluous.

- *Bring/take.* You bring something toward you and take it away. You take money to the store and bring home groceries.

- *By.* Often unnecessary, as in "revenues last quarter increased by 3 percent." You simply don't need to include the *by*.

- *Close proximity.* Redundant. *Proximity* includes the idea of closeness.

- *Coequal.* Lawyers may like it, but it's redundant.

- *Could care less.* Just plain wrong. The total indifference this phrase is going for means you could *not* care less.

- *Criteria*. A plural word that takes a plural verb.

- *Data*. Same as *criteria*.

- *Decimate*. Technically from the old Roman custom of an army commander killing every tenth soldier as a means of keeping discipline in the ranks. It doesn't mean annihilation, just significant destruction.

- *Dialogue*. It's a noun, not a verb, and certainly not a transitive verb. You can't "dialogue this." You can have a dialogue about this. Or better, you can talk about it.

- *Do the math*. Overused. If I had a nickel for every time I've heard this, well, do the math.

- *Each and every*. Redundant and trite.

- *Fewer/less*. Use *fewer* if there is a number involved. *Less* refers to a volume. So, for instance, "in ten words or less" is wrong.

- *First*, as in *"first announced."* *Announce* means that it hasn't been made public before. Therefore the use of *first* is redundant.

- *Free gift*. All gifts are free; otherwise they are not gifts.

- *Future potential*. The word *potential* includes the concept of futurity. You can't have past potential.

- *Gather together*. Redundant. *Gather* includes the concept of bringing people or things together.

- *Going forward*. Vastly overused and usually superfluous. "We will be expanding our product base" says it all; no need for the "going forward" too many people tack on to such statements.

- *Hopefully.* Wrong: "Hopefully we'll get it right this time." Right: "We hope we'll get it right this time." *Hopefully*, an adverb, should be next to the verb it modifies, as in, "We entered the contest hopefully."

- *Importantly.* It's not technically correct to say, "Just as importantly . . ." *Importantly* connotes self-pride, as in "he sashayed into the room importantly, yet no one looked." In most cases, use "Just as important" instead.

- *In a half hour from now*—often said by radio announcers and emcees talking about upcoming events. Lose the "from now." It's captured in the word *in.*

- *In his lifetime.* As in "One in eight men will develop prostate cancer in his lifetime." There has never been a case of prebirth or posthumous prostate cancer. The phrase is unnecessary.

- *In order to.* Wordy. As is "so as to"; a simple *to* is enough.

- *Irregardless.* No such word.

- *Join together. Join* means "bring together," so you don't need both. You cannot join apart. (See also *Gather together*.)

- *Leverage our strengths.* Wrong on so many levels. First, *leverage* is a noun. You don't leverage something, you lever it. And why in the world would you lever your weaknesses? That's a losing strategy for sure.

- *Literally.* A tricky one because the word literally means what it says. It is wrong to say, "We literally sliced the provisioning time in half" if you didn't actually take a knife or a scalpel to it. However, if you say, "We sliced the provisioning time literally in half," it's all right because the *literally* in this case refers to the time, not the slicing. Most times, just leave it out.

- *Low-hanging fruit.* Overused.

- *Near miss.* Not really. When planes just avoid colliding, it's not a near miss. It's an actual miss. It's a near hit. But whoever heard of that? Avoid the use when possible.

- *Needless to say.* If so, why say it?

- *Only.* Put it right in front of the word it modifies. "I only cry at night" means you do nothing but cry at night; you don't sleep, eat, read, breathe. Probably you mean "I cry only at night."

- *Plan ahead.* It would be silly to plan behind, wouldn't it?

- *Preplan.* What does this mean? Plan to plan? Planning is planning. There is no pre.

- *Presently.* Means "in a little while," not "now." If you want to say "now," use "now."

- *Protest against. Protest* includes in its definition the idea of opposition. You can demonstrate in favor of something, but you cannot protest in favor. Drop the *against.*

- *Left the company to pursue other interests.* Everyone knows the person was fired. An embarrassingly transparent euphemism. Put a period after *company.*

- *Surrounded on all sides. Surrounded* means all around you. *On all sides* is redundant.

- *The both of.* It's just "both."

- *Think to myself.* Unless, like Kreskin, you can actually project your thoughts, you cannot help but think to yourself.

- *Unique.* This is a word that cannot be modified. It means one of a kind. It cannot be very, or almost, or somewhat. It is what it is: unique.

- *Very.* Almost always a useless word. Much too wishy-washy to convey true depth of commitment; too common to provide the listener with any image of the comparative nature of your comment. "It is very cold" pales beside any statement such as "It is as cold as New Year's Day in Nebraska."

- *Whether or not.* In its definition, the word *whether* includes the "or not." Therefore the "or not" is superfluous, wordy, redundant—you name it.

- *Young child.* Redundant.

Authorities may differ on some of these points. And many have much longer lists of troublesome words—book-length lists, in fact. What's important is to pay attention to the details in your writing so that your audience isn't detoured, even for a moment, from the path you intend they take with you. Write your speech to follow the direct path to their attention and to their memory.

Key Points

- Write simply. Simple words. Short sentences.

- Avoid jargon and clichés.

- Use quotations judiciously.

- Your title is your first impression—make a good one.

- Use the right word; almost is not close enough.

Note

1. From Remarks at the Poor Richard Club, Philadelphia, 1985, in *The 2003 Speechwriter's Conference Handbook* (Chicago: Ragan Communications, 2003).
  2. Ibid.

Of Headlines, Humor, and "Aha!s"

Now that you're an expert on grammar and simple language, now that you have the courage not to lean on quotations or word slides, there are still a few important elements to consider when writing your speech. It's fundamentally important to visualize the responses your speech will evoke, both in the room and in the broader world. Once you've "seen" where you want to go, you can build the milestones and signposts into what you say.

Part of that is to weigh carefully your use of humor. It's often an easy way to connect with an audience and relax yourself. But it is also a risky tool in the mouth of the inexperienced. And then, when you have your words all written down, there is the issue of approvals, of guiding your beloved text through the cadres of subject-matter experts, confidants, and bosses you have used as your sounding board, your checks and balances.

This chapter takes a look at all those issues, beginning with strategies to get the response you envision.

Provide the Aha! Moment

Remember this old line? The stand-up comic is dying on stage. His airplane food jokes are stale. His Los Angeles freeway stories have stalled. No one will take his wife, please, and thank you. He looks out into the spotlight and tries one more: "What is this, an audience or an oil painting?"

The truth is that many speakers would rather be talking to an oil painting than to living, breathing, and especially thinking human beings. That's why, so often, speakers rattle through their text as if they were in a hurry to catch the last flight of the Concorde. That's why they don't look up. Or hide in plain sight beside the slides. But in doing so, they forget that, fundamentally, a speech is not a monologue.

"What do you mean? There's only one person talking. What else would you call it?" How about a virtual dialogue?

Too often, we think that, given a roomful of people and a podium, all we have to do is get up and talk. The audience is there to listen, so they will listen. And they will understand. Listen? Well, let's assume that most of them will listen, at least most of the time. The question is, will they actually hear—and understand—what you're saying? The answer is not necessarily yes, for the act of hearing is exactly that: an action requiring more than just the physiological capability of an intact eardrum and functioning saddlebone in the ear. It requires actively engaging in the words and ideas that are flowing from your mouth.

The same is true with understanding, which is more than just hearing. It's engagement. The audience will hear what the speaker is saying and assess it in relation to everything that they—as individuals—know. In fact, their perception will be affected by everything that they are and have experienced: their schooling, their on-the-job experience, their diverse personalities, their learning style preferences, their disparate value systems, even the state of their digestive system. All these are part of the context they bring to your words, context that is acting on your ideas, influencing the audience's understanding of—and ultimately their agreement with—the points you are making.

Test yourself on this one. Next time you're listening to someone give a speech, try to watch yourself listen to the speech. I suspect you'll find there will be points at which you mentally nod your head in agreement and other moments where you would like to say, "Hey, wait a second there . . . I don't quite buy that leap of faith." At still other times, you could well be lost: "Where the heck is she going with this . . . ?" And, I would hope, at the end, you're saying to yourself, "Okay, I get it. Not bad, not bad at all."

If you can't do it inside your own head, pick a seat where you can watch the audience to see how they're bringing their own experiential whole to play as they engage in hearing the speech. You can actually see brows furrow and eyes roll at some questionable points, a quick consultation with a neighbor when an obscure point fails to hit home, heads nod when the speaker strikes a common note. Sometimes you can even see the lips move.

This is decidedly not an oil painting out there. This is an audience. They're asking questions of themselves as you talk, comparing your observations with their own. They're totting up the good points you make versus the objections they have. They're asking questions to clarify. They're laughing and nodding, not off, but in agreement or even just in contemplation. Any speech—good or bad—will elicit reactions like this. But a great speech, a memorable speech, will orchestrate those reactions, like a great play. Playwrights live to engage their audiences. They work to evoke responses, and for the most part, they want those responses to be predictable. That means they must be managed, which means, in the most crass terms, they must be planted.

Great playwrights look for the lines that will guarantee a laugh, open the tear ducts, or unleash the screams. They build to them, acknowledging that the audience reaction is as much a part of the play as the script itself. In the same way, a great speech acknowledges the essential participation of the audience as the intellectually and emotionally involved partner in the proceedings, albeit a silent one.

So it is up to you to write a speech that manages, to the extent possible, the responses. As you write, try to build in natural response points and "Aha!" moments when all of a sudden the obscuring clouds clear and the insight gleams forth like a ray of sunlight. It can even mean breaking the fourth wall, as they say in theater. That's the invisible barrier that separates audience from actor on stage. Young drama students have pounded into them from their first open house in front of the parents that they should never break the fourth wall. They must find a focus within the confines of the stage and not play up to Mom and Dad. Some actors, mostly comics like Carol Burnett and Mike Myers, break through the fourth wall to great effect occasionally, mugging shamelessly to bring the audience in even closer to the tomfoolery in which they are engaged.

The same tactic works well for speakers, used sparingly of course. That doesn't include the mugging, for that is by and large unseemly from an executive. But breaking the fourth wall makes the connection, acknowledging the audience's key role in actively responding to the speech. Rhetorical questions are an easy and effective way to do that. They acknowledge that the speaker has an idea what the listener may be thinking. For example: "So the Stephens Island wren holds the distinction of being the only species ever wiped out by a single household cat. 'So what?' I can almost hear you say. Well, let me tell you what."

There are other ways to draw the audience directly in., for instance by putting into words the thoughts you believe may be in their heads: "I see some raised eyebrows. So I'm thinking some of you may be a bit skeptical of that last bit. So let me put it to you this way . . ." Or this: "I can almost hear you thinking that this is not what I came here to hear. Well, yes and no. . . ."

Interesting, surprise twists to a story also provide many an "Aha!" moment. News commentator Paul Harvey made a pretty good living out of this device in his oral essays called The Rest of the Story. He'd start a long tale about some obscure person, a story that wound its way seemingly to nowhere for a couple of minutes. Then, after the commercial break, which also featured Paul Harvey, came the kicker. "That nobody I've been talking about? She turned out to be the mother of Mike Nesmith, the guitarist of the Monkees. . . . but more than that, she also changed the world for secretaries when she invented Liquid Paper." Aha!!

This Paul Harvey technique works best when you have a good story to tell about yourself or your organization. My old boss was once making a speech to an audience of salespeople who were facing a real uphill challenge in a tough market. A man who almost forced his optimistic outlook to come true, he wanted to speak about making the impossible possible. But this audience had recently been squeezed out of a series of big sales deals and were in no mood for platitudes.

As luck would have it, my boss had started his career with a company that makes the trailer part of tractor-trailer rigs. In one of his first deals, he lost a major account to the company's fiercest competitor. He went to his boss filled with dread of having to pass on the horrible news, as the lost contract was a big one that would be in force for years. He told the boss that he'd tried everything to get the sale, but the deal was final. It was impossible to get into this customer. His boss listened quietly and then said, "Okay, here's what you do. Get the plant to make up the best damn trailer possible and then have it delivered to the customer free of charge. With it, send a note that says, 'This is one of our products. When the competitor's trailers begin to break down, which they will, put ours on the road, for free, with no obligation, and then see what you think.'"

Well, of course, the competitors' trailers lasted awhile, so the suspense in the story could be built up. But finally one day, my friend got a call from the customer. The customer's chosen trailers had broken down, they had tried the free one and were now ready to renegotiate. "Aha!" The light went on for the people in the room. They all got it at the same time, and—at least at that moment—they all reacted as we had planned. They went back into the field reenergized, with a new wrinkle to add to the mythical stature of the big boss. Objective met.

Build in the Headline

Another technique to get you to your Golden Goals of being memorable is to borrow a trick from elite athletes who visualize the result before making the play. In this context, I'm talking about writing in some headlines you'd like to see in any news story about your speech. These headlines not only give any media a pretty unsubtle hint about where you think the story lies, they also provide convenient, signposts to help your audience along as you speak.

By their nature, headlines are attention grabbers. They summarize in pithy language a whole bunch of words and ideas and facts. They are, in a story-telling sense, not the headline but the bottom line: *what should be remembered*. As such, they are essential for helping the immediate audience understand your speech in the moment, and more important, remember it past the next bathroom break.

Headlines act as signposts. "This is where we are" (or in the South, "This is where we're at.") They act as summaries and conclusions. They act as transitions. Okay, part one is over; on to the next part of this. Most important, headlines are memory hooks.

"I am not a crook."

"Let them come to Berlin."

"I did not . . . (whatever) . . . with that woman."

"A thousand points of light."

We remember the words. And we remember the whole bucket of issues that surrounded them. Will we ever say anything as memorable? Chances are, no. It's unlikely we'll be called upon to speak of such issues of historical moment on the grand stage of life. Could happen, but it's unlikely. But it doesn't matter. You still want to stand out within the context of your own environment, on matters of moment for you. And you do *that* by being memorable. By giving your audience help to remember you. Hooks like headlines, with sharp points.

Often the headlines will be among the last things you write, after you've worked your way through your research, arrived at your thesis, and told your story. In some cases, the headline will jump out at you from the prose you've put on the page. Other times, they take work. My suggestion is to start with the main point you want the audience to remember, however you've expressed it. Then whittle it down to no more than a handful of words, especially short words. Yes, you may lose something in the translation, but it's only temporary—the rest of your talk will illuminate and elucidate. And the point is to oversimplify to be memorable.

Imagery, simile, and metaphor can work wonders in creating a memorable headline. So can common idioms. For example: "This policy opens a real can of worms." Just as often, though, it's a simple declaratory statement in plain language: "Read my lips."

Headlines, of course, do more than act as signposts for the audience. They also ratchet up your ability to get the kind of media coverage you want, if that is one of your objectives. The rule here is that if you want the media to give prominence to your position, give them what they need. And what they need is headlines, whether it's for the top of a story in the paper, or on the ubiquitous text crawl at the bottom of the screen on all the big television news networks.

You see the power of the headline all the time when major figures give big speeches, and goodness knows we've had a lot of those since 9/11. Watch any of the cable news networks cover a presidential or Cabinet-level speech. Every couple of minutes, in a box below the live feed of the speaker, you'll see mini-headlines of what the person has said just two or three minutes before. And the crawl below that will have even more, to be repeated in a seemingly endless loop for the next few hours.

So write the headlines into the talk. It makes it much easier for the reporter to pick out what's important from your perspective. And who doesn't like someone else to help make their job easier? And clearly, despite the failings of the Fifth Estate, the media are an essential audience for your message. After all, gaining attention for yourself and your organization is the point of the whole exercise, isn't it? And like them or not, there is nothing that gets to more of that public more often and more effectively than the media. Media coverage is more than just spreading the message. It also is tantamount to third-party recognition, if not endorsement. Editors and producers of mainstream media are, believe it or not, paid to be discerning about what constitutes legitimate news, the focus on Michael Jackson's bedroom habits notwithstanding.

If your speech gets printed in the local daily, or covered on Eyewitness News, people know it has gone through at least some intellectual filters in the newsroom and been deemed a point of view worthy of getting some attention. These media outlets are not Web sites or blogs that spew out reams of material with no discernible critical limits in sight. They are a part of an establishment institution. Granted, it's a raffish and often infuriating institution, but it is no less an integral part of legitimate public discourse.

So when the media pick up part of your speech, that act alone gives you credibility you didn't have before you made the speech.

When writing in your own headlines, keep in mind that nuance is not a strong suit of the media. There is always too much news to fit on the page or in the time slot. It's a fact of life that is galling to people who spend their careers negotiating their way through the subtleties and complexities of life's issues. Invariably after a brush with the media, these people feel like icebergs, with only a small fraction of their substance breaking the surface in any media treatment. But it is a fact of life.

Your fact of life is that you want fair coverage that reflects the depth and breadth of your thinking. So when you begin the writing process—in fact, when you set your objectives—envision the best possible headline you might achieve from the appearance. Imagine the photo accompanying the article, a dramatic shot from below the lectern up to you gesticulating passionately, with a six-word cutline perfectly capturing your main message. "Payroll tax ties entreprenuers' hands, SME guru charges." Or think about the clip on the local TV news. You're not going to get much more than six seconds to make your point. So which six seconds of your twenty minutes do you want the video editor to choose?

Oh yes, headlines count, so write the headlines into the talk. But let's be clear about one thing. The media won't always be in attendance, and even if they are, they may not be interested. A lot depends on external factors outside your control, like maybe someone else at the conference has invented the better mouse-trap, or some rogue leader somewhere has dropped the big one. You can't compete with that. You can only do your best.

On the Lighter Side

Know what the six most frightening words in any speech are? My vote goes to these: "That reminds me of a story. . . ."

Jokers Beware

Used to be, many how-to books about giving speeches sug-gested that it was a good idea to open a speech with a joke. Who doesn't like a laugh, they said. More important, a joke acts like the overture at a musical—it's a bit of a tease for the performance to come. It also gives the audience a chance to get settled in their chairs, unwrap their cough drops, whisper to their neighbor about the stage setting, or your tie, or their plans for later. More than that, people almost expect it. So when they hear you launch into a joke, they relax a bit, knowing they're on familiar ground. And it gives the ushers time to seat the guests who, inevitably, are too rude and self-involved to think that their late arrival might inconvenience others and spoil the carefully crafted opening mo-ment.

It also has to be said that telling a joke can be a real plus for the speaker. A joke humanizes you, lets all those people out there beyond the footlights know that you're a regular person, not some holier- or mightier-than-thou shadow watcher. There's a physiological plus, too. Most of us are dead scared to open our mouths in front of a roomful of strangers. So in anticipation of the talk, our nerves get frayed beyond the normal stress levels experienced by astronauts in the centrifuge machine. In response, our adrenal glands open up like the Grand Coulee Dam just as we stride to the podium. And for the first 30 seconds, we're ready to chew the scenery.

But that feeling passes quickly, and once the initial adrenaline rush ends, our nerves take over again, our breath gets short, chests tighten, palms get sweaty. Telling a joke gets you through all that—it gets you warmed up, and when the audience laughs uproariously, you have time to take a deep breath and calm down again. As they pick themselves off the floor, you get the sense that, hey, this will be all right. They seem to like you. And you can almost feel your pulse rate return to the low triple digits, if not below.

So what's your beef, Carlson? Well, lots of them, actually. First, why on earth, if you want to be remembered, would you start with the expected? Why open with the hoariest cliché of all? First impressions count most, and telling a joke is ordinary. That's not where you want to end up, so why would you choose that as the place you start? Especially when there are dozens of other, better ways to get into whatever it is you have to say.

Just as important, humor is one of the most intensely subjective things known to humankind—especially in these politically correct days. Blonde jokes, lawyer jokes, Polish jokes, one-eyed hunchback jokes. Try one, and you're sure to offend some part of your audience. Even if there are no blondes around, someone will be offended that you would assume to stereotype a person. One man's Jerry Seinfeld is another one's Dick Cheney . . . and vice versa.

I once wrote a set of presentations for a company's annual employee kickoff meeting. One per vice-president, laying out the accomplishments of the year before and the plan for the year to come. Pretty mundane stuff, made even more so by the fact that I had not yet met any of these people but was asked to create 20-minute segments for each of them based on their units' business plans. No one thought the audience would have trouble sitting through six straight recitations, plus the chairman's vision-thing message. "This is the blueprint for our business," they said in the lead-up to the event. "People will be interested."

On the day, of course, eyes were glazing over before the first VP finished his sixth slide on priorities for 1998 or 1997—so memorable, not even the year sticks in my brain. To his credit, the sales VP, who was speaking fourth, sensed the audience was drifting a bit—after all, it had been three hours since the event began because, of course, they had to run videos after every speaker to vary the pace.

Now this VP was a bit of an aging frat boy type—not uncommon in the sales field. He was some fun to be around in a bar or a locker room or even in the wings of an award show dinner. But sometimes, he lost sight of the limits of his charm. This was one such case. Determined to break the monotonous litany of good intentions that was putting the crowd to sleep, he decided to open with a joke. It was a farmer's daughter-type joke, risqué if not downright ribald. In fact, it was a good joke. Funny in the locker room, or after a few beers. But in this room, with this audience, it tanked.

As he told it, many people in the audience looked at each other, asking with their eyes, "Is he really telling that kind of joke, here, in mixed company, in a business meeting?" They continued to be distracted throughout his talk. After, in the reception, people were asking the same question, only this time with their voices. Oh yes, he made an impression that day. He was memorable. But not for anything of substance that he had to say. Only for his farmer's daughter joke.

It's hard to ever take anyone seriously after a gaffe like that. It's a real shot to his credibility as a leader, as an executive who needs to demonstrate judgment, even as a sensitive person. So the content of a joke is problematic. The best jokes always cut closest to the bone. But in a world where tribal differences are very much in vogue, at a time when everyone is very much on orange alert for insults to their interests, cutting to the bone can leave your brand without a leg to stand on.

This is especially true when you're in front of international audiences, for a good shaggy dog story in America could well be an insult to members of the audience from another cultural background. Consider this transcript of a translator relaying an executive's speech to an audience in Japan:

> American businessman is beginning speech with thing called joke. I am not certain why, but all American businessmen believe it necessary to start speech with joke. [pause] He is telling joke now, but frankly, you wouldn't understand it, so I won't translate it. He thinks I am telling you the joke now. [*pause*] The polite thing to do when he finishes is to laugh. [*pause*] He is getting close. [*pause*] Now! [*audience laughs*]." After the speech, the executive was all over the translator with praise: "You are the first translator who knows how to tell a good joke."[1]

'Nuff said.

And telling a joke isn't just about the joke. It's also about the telling. And not everyone can tell a joke well. There's timing involved. Inflection. Spontaneity. It is a killer, isn't it, when the speaker gets up and *reads* the joke. But I bet you've seen it done.

There's an episode in the old *Dick Van Dyke Show* in which Dick and his team of comedy writers are forced to write a stand-up routine for the son of a mob boss. Amidst much nervous hilarity, the team comes up with some pretty good material, including one bit about a train conductor ("What's a train conductor, Daddy?") with allergies who has to stifle his sneezes as he announces the station stops. When Dick delivers a line like, "Next stop, Sch . . . Sch . . Schen . . . Schenectady!" using his rubber face and equally flexible pencil-thin body, it's pretty funny. Then watch the ultra-earnest wannabe comic Kenny Dexter, complete with mob heavies as bodyguards. "Next stop, Schenectady," says Kenny. "Achoo." Better make that "Next Stop, Not Funny."

Good material can't save bad delivery. People who tell jokes for a living worry as much or more about the delivery as they do about the substance. Look at Leno, who learned from Carson. When one of his monologue jokes hits a wall of silence, he can still get a laugh just by his reaction to the dead air. More than that, he uses his body, his foil (the bandleader), the little step on his stage . . . anything else he can think of to sell the material. Bob Hope did the same thing. One big difference between them and us is that they have a bank of goodwill on which to draw when a given bit fails. Leno's audience thinks he's funny because they've seen him be funny, over and over. So they can forgive the odd flat one because they know there'll be another good one along soon. As a speaker, you simply don't have that reservoir to draw on. If you're known to your audience at all, chances are it is not as a comedian—at least not an intentional comedian. So you can't afford to fall flat. As Eminem says, "You've only got one shot. Do not miss your chance."

Telling jokes looks easy and even feels easy in some circumstances. "Hell, I'm the life of our office parties with some of my gags. All the people who work for me think my jokes are hilarious." Of course they do. "I can just write something funny, then stand up there and say it." Oh really? The fact is, it only *looks* easy because Leno and others like him are professionals. You don't expect to golf like Tiger Woods, do you? So why would you expect to be able to master the art of telling a joke? My advice is that jokes in speeches should come with the same warning that car commercials put in small type as the stunt driver slaloms to the edge of the Grand Canyon: "Professionals Only. Do not try this at home."

Let alone on a podium. At least not until you've tried out your material and your delivery in a comedy club in North Pine Bluff. Otherwise, you run the risk of injury—to your personal brand if not your ego.

Humor Is Another Matter

Now, let's be clear. While jokes are, for me, pretty much verboten, humor is not. A witty person would be doing herself a disfavor if her ability to elicit a smile or even a guffaw was stunted in the name of "serious subject matter." Even the most weighty material can usually use a lightener here and there, if only to vary the tone, pitch, and pace of the presentation. The use of the well-placed one-liner, or inside joke, can let the audience know very quickly that the speaker has some intellectual hops, as a roundball fan might say.

In fact, I'm a great fan of what you might call the Simpsons Principle. I suspect very few people alive—or dead for that matter—get every one of the thousands of pop culture throw-away references made during the course of a season of this so-called cartoon show. Some of them are obvious; some are groaners, as we used to call heavy-handed puns. But some are so clever that you just shake your head at the associations they bring forth. So you don't want to shake your head too long or you'll miss the next one.

A.O. Scott, writing in *The New York Times,* describes one such moment when Bart is wandering through Manhattan and comes to the office of *MAD* magazine:

> "When he asks the surly receptionist if he can take a tour, she shoos him away. 'There's nothing to see here, Sonny.' But just as Bart is about to leave, Alfred E. Neuman himself pokes his head through the door, spouting vaudevillian mock Yiddish. Behind him is a chaotic room in which the pages of the magazine seem to have come to life, as if the drawings of Don Martin and Dave Berg's 'Lighter Side' were simple, faithful renderings of the world the artists inhabited. 'Wow,' says Bart, 'I'll never wash these eyes again.'"[2]

That's evocative for all those devotees of the magazine, of course. But also a tremendously sly dig at people who just don't get the joy of goofiness, either in *MAD* or in *The Simpsons*.

Now for many viewers of that episode, the reference would be lost. My daughters, for instance, now young women, had no idea who Alfred E. Neuman is. So the bit wasn't as rich for them as for those of us who actually grew up trying to figure out in advance what the joke would be when you folded the inside back cover in upon itself. But for those of us who did waste all those hours with Spy vs. Spy, we had, for a moment at least, common ground with the Simpsons.

The same goes for making subtle connections in speeches. When I'm writing anything, but especially an article or a speech, I try to throw in something that not everyone will get or even notice. It's a pleasant enough game for me, and if anyone does notice it, I like to think they'll be impressed with the my subtle wit, or eclectic knowledge base. I can be as simple as a bit of alliteration or a reference to a Dan Hicks song—you know, of Dan Hicks and His Hot Licks fame. The point is that you should try to sprinkle some leaven on the loaf of your speech. And you need not explain every word. It's all right if some references, some witty lines, bypass some members of the audience. It's all right if only a few people really get the connection between Bart (which is an anagram for brat, by the way) and Koestler's definition of humor as the collision of contexts. There will still be plenty of grain for the multitudes. It's just that the cream of the crop—who, one likes to think, will be the leaders and influencers in the mob—get a little extra.

Finally, when it comes to humor, a little self-deprecation goes a long way to make a solid connection with the audience. It lets them know that you put your pants on one leg at a time, that some days you do wear socks from two different pairs, that you have to jump through some of the same human hoops that they do just to get through the day. It shows a sense of humility, always attractive, and a degree of perspective that charms and disarms the audience. But it isn't without risk. For if the ear is hearing humility and the eye is seeing an arrogant patrician who wouldn't know how to get on a bus, the effect will not be positive.

If you don't know anything about sports, you shouldn't tell a sports anecdote. If you've never added a can of tuna to some macaroni and cheese to make a quick casserole, you shouldn't really talk too long about how tough it is to make ends meet on a six-figure salary, what with Ivy League tuition for the kids being what it is. If you've never had to buy shoes at a Wal-Mart, don't brag about roughing it at the family cottage.

Self-directed humor has to have authenticity. People have to believe that you could get yourself into the situations you describe. It's possible to fake authenticity, but not forever. If it's not really part of you, people will find out. And then not only are you a crumby story teller, you're also down a quart in the credibility reservoir in everything else you do.

Having said all this about jokes and humor, I would just remind you that there is a time and place for everything. And you may well be asked to speak at an event where telling a joke up front is absolutely the right thing to do. It will probably be a less formal event, one in which you are on some higher level of intimacy with the audience than a normal keynote speaker might be. Since you ask, a good measuring stick is if you know more than half of them by their first names or if you've seen a good portion of them naked in the shower. This sort of thing greatly broadens the latitude you can take with general guidelines. And gives you more insight into the kind of joke they might like.

Beyond that, however, there are other times when a joke just fits, when it's apropos the topic at hand or unexpected in the circumstances—like Chris Rock giving the eulogy at a funeral. For example, I was once asked to pen the words for a senior executive to give at a gathering of heavy thinkers in the telecommunications industry. The topic was the regulation of the sector. The client was to make the case that the regulatory regime had been appropriate when designed ten years prior, but it was no longer, given the surge of the Internet and the evolution of technology so that cable television companies as well as Internet voice companies could compete with telephone companies to deliver voice telephony services to customers.

This was a very serious topic: companies with billions of sunk assets facing an uncertain future; upstarts trying to overcome the stigma of the dot-gone disaster. There would be industry executives and regulators and government supremos in the audience. "Time for a joke," says I. Well, not quite. But almost.

I had a tremendous amount of information from the speaker and his staff on the key points he wanted to make. Some of them he'd made before in articles I'd ghosted for him. But from my point of view, we had no entry point and no connection with the audience. Then, about six weeks before the speech was to be given, I was vegging out at the end of the day in front of the television, flipping through our 500-channel universe. Lo and behold, who was on Jay Leno but George Carlin? More surprising, he didn't get interviewed by Jay right away but rather he first did a standup bit of about six minutes. He told a lot of jokes, but one made me both laugh out loud and then think, "Hey, good line."

I went to bed without incident—I say that only to shorten the story, not to comment on my usual ability to get to bed—but when I got back to work the next morning, the joke was still in my mind. As I puzzled over my voluminous notes for the speech, I had one of those Eureka moments. And this is what I wrote:

> A few weeks ago I happened to catch George Carlin on Jay Leno's Tonight Show. Now if you've seen George lately, you know that, like a lot of us, he looks a *bit* older than he did when his claim to fame was the list of seven words one couldn't say on TV. I'm not going to say what words were on that list. But judging from what I hear on TV these days, the List of Seven seems to have shrunk to zero.
>
> That may say something about the changing nature of regulation. But it's only tangentially my point. Because George has new material. And one line in particular caught my attention the other night because it speaks to one of the key challenges we face in our industry today.
>
> "Some people say the glass is half full," George said. "Some people say the glass is half empty.

"But I say," and here he paused for effect, "but I say the glass is too *big*!"

It's the oldest trick in a comedian's bag, right? Take a common-place observation. Twist it slightly. Take the received wisdom of the day. Ask the oddball question. Get a laugh. But a laugh that comes with a sense of "Gee, I never thought about it that way before."

It's all about changing the perspective. As surely as if you turned your binoculars around to look through the big lenses. And, in so doing, gained new insight.

> As a relatively new kid on this block, I come to work every day blessed with the opportunity to ask the oddball questions. It's easier for me to have a different perspective.
>
> In my ignorance—and I use that word in its most positive sense, of course—I am able (even compelled) to question the received wisdom, much like a two-year-old will pester Mom and Dad with an endless string of "whys."
>
> That's what I've done for the last eight or nine months as I brought myself up to speed on the regulatory issues facing this sector. My sense of the answers I've heard is that, too often, we act as if we were still back in the days of yore, when George Carlin was the Hippy Dippy Weatherman.
>
> I'm coming to believe that the real issue is not whether we have too much regulation . . . or too little. The real question is this: Is our regulatory glass the right size for the way the technology is evolving and, most important, for the way ordinary people are using the technologies we're putting in their hands? And my answer is no.
>
> We must shift our perspective. We must look again at

the relative importance of this sector to the growth of our economy, of our country. And we must make the fundamental adjustments to nurture that development. We must right-size the glass.

No question, we started the speech with a joke. But it was a joke integrally linked with the thesis. What made it even better was the fact that Carlin himself became famous fighting regulatory oversight that had not kept up with the community mores of that era. It was a joke that revealed a bit of this speaker's lively personality . . . and the fact that he has a few annual rings around his trunk. It humanized not only the speaker, but also a very technical and difficult set of issues. And all because I can't get to sleep before midnight.

As I said, there is a time and place for everything. But if you're going to open with a joke, please make sure the time and place are, indeed, right.

Gaining Approval

Imagine if you will that Franklin Delano Roosevelt sent his post–Pearl Harbor address out to a wide range of colleagues for approval before he delivered it. "I like it, FDR, but . . . day of infamy? What the hell's infamy? Nobody knows what that means. How about 'historic day'?"

Or imagine that Winston Churchill went through a similar process when he spoke about the possibility of Britain giving up in the Second World War. "Winnie. Jolly good stuff, old man. But I think you may have gone a bit overboard with the 'we shall never, never, never, never, never, never surrender' piece. Perhaps one 'never' would be more appropriate to your position as prime minister."

Thankfully, the philistines did not get their hands on these great pieces of rhetoric. But it could happen, and does with great regularity in corporations all over the world. While companies do not pay as much attention to a speech as they do to a fifteen-second radio commercial, it's still true that a number of senior eyes—and red pencils—pass over any speech of enough significance. Many if not most senior executives make it a practice to send drafts to their trusted lieutenants or colleagues, seeking to test their ideas, uncover land mines, check the facts.

All that is as it should be. No writer can know where all the skeletons lie. No one can keep up with the way facts and even figures change within otherwise stable companies. If you've ever gone through the process of developing material to report on end-of-quarter results, you know that figures can change as the deadline approaches, not through any malfeasance, but because results keep getting updated as various outposts are heard from and as interpretations of what goes where are finalized. Most often, the changes are miniscule, a single digit here and there, often to the right of the decimal point. But the end product must be right.

In principle, the idea of circulating a speech for comment is a sound one. It's in the execution that trouble lies. There are a couple of reasons for that. First is the unavoidable fact of the human character: If you ask someone to comment on a piece of written material, he or she will comment—and not just on his or her area of expertise.

The great thing about writing is that everybody can do it. Everybody has to prepare reports, send off e-mails, even write a letter from time to time. "Can't be hard. I speak English; all I have to do is put down what I would say on paper."

Some people are accomplished writers in their field of expertise—or at least they think so. Lawyers come to mind. They work hard and carefully to develop cogent, watertight prose that will cement an argument. Cogent, yes, but not necessarily clear. And not necessarily written for the ear. But that doesn't stop them, or anyone else, from having opinions, often loud and very firm opinions, about the writing done by others.

Writers themselves are perhaps the worst culprits. Give me a piece of someone else's deathless prose, and I'll have my editing pencil in hand so fast the top of my ear will burn from the friction. I love to use the tool in the word processing program that not only lets me show where I've edited stuff, but also allows me to insert comments so that the writer knows exactly why my way of saying things is so much better.

So the draft text goes out to the trusted few for comments, usually by tomorrow, please. And what comes back, over the next three or four days is a flurry of comments on everything from "make sure you use the most up-to-date numbers" to stylistic suggestions. In the Stephens Island speech I referred to earlier, I had carefully crafted a strong central metaphor. About four or five times through the speech, I referred back to the metaphor briefly, with just a couple of words. "Remember the Stephens Island wren." Or "That's the Stephens Island wren writ large." One vice-president was not impressed: "Why do we keep repeating this stuff about the wren?" he wrote in his marginalia. "Too much wren!"

Well, everyone is entitled to his opinion. But he missed the point. These references served multiple purposes: They reinforced the central, organizing metaphor; they served as a verbal signal that one section of the argument was over and another about to begin; they enabled the speaker to pause and take a breath; and they enabled the members of the audience also to pause and assimilate the ideas for a second, or reconnect if they'd zoned out for a couple of minutes. Very useful little things. But lost on this particular commentator because he did not have the expertise to recognize what he was reading.

That's not to say he shouldn't be asked to comment. Only that the request should be made clear: "Here is what I propose to say in my speech to the upcoming national conference on interconnectivity and hyper-convergence. Please review to ensure we are using the correct data and the appropriate inferences we draw from them." He will still, more than likely, try to wordsmith the piece. But he cannot have the same level of expectation that his changes on other matters will see the light of day in the final product.

And that brings me to the second execution issue in terms of getting approvals and comments. And it is this: The more people who feel they have standing in the speech-creation process, the more people whose wording changes are accepted, the less likely it is that the speech will hang together as a piece of communication. After all, you know what designed the elephant. A committee. And when was the last time you remember reading or hearing anything written by a committee that you thought was well written? Not recently, I'm betting.

That's why State of the Union addresses are generally not memorable. They are laundry lists of bullet points with wording submitted verbatim by various branches of government all wanting to get their oars wet. No question, key stakeholders must have their say on the substantive issues of positioning, of factual accuracy, even of emphasis. But in the end, to have the memorable impact you need, the speech must come from you. Issues of which word to use, which example to highlight, which metaphor to hang your ideas on—all these are properly up to you alone. And you cannot allow good tight prose to be deadened with the inevitable disclaimers and qualifiers that people who thrive in hierarchies are so insistent on.

This is not counsel to be reckless. Far from it. It is counsel to be clear and declarative. To be memorable. To leave endless equivocation to others. You want to stand out? Own the words. And make each one count. Do not be talked into watering down your message by people who will not be standing up there on the podium, trying to make a lasting impression on a roomful of strangers.

Key Points

- Build in the headlines, the natural response points—and the Aha! moments.

- Handle humor with care. Opt for wit over jokes.

- Use quotations sparingly, if at all.

- Put checks on those who check your writing.

Notes

1. As quoted in Roger E. Axtell and John P. Healy, *Do's and Taboos of Hosting International Visitors* (New York: Wiley, 1994). Cited as January 5, 2004 entry in Ross & Kathryn Petras, *The 365 Stupidest Things Ever Said Page-a-Day Calendar* (New York: Workman Publishing Company, 2004).

2. A.O. Scott, "How 'The Simpsons' Survives," *The New York Times* (November 4, 2001).

Showtime

Only connect! Only connect the prose and the passion and both will be exalted.

—E.M. Forster

Before You Say a Word

It's all in place now. Venue secured, research done, text written. There's nothing to do but stand on the dais and deliver. Nothing indeed! As crazy old King Lear said, "Nothing will come of nothing." And there is many a slip betwixt the word processor and the word enunciator, between the written page and the spoken word.

So there are a few things left to do to make sure your attempt to be memorable actually pays off. Let's start with mundane stuff, like how the words appear on the page.

Big Type, Lots of White Space

I can never remember if, with increasing age, eyesight is the first or second thing to go. Maybe it's memory. But the peepers surely do fade, and thousands of optometrists are the richer for it. Reach a certain—ah, stature in life—and the fine print fuzzes over. Even the 12-point type in the newspaper is a little more difficult to decipher over the morning decaf.

Imagine trying to read that type in a darkened room with a thousand-watt spotlight in your face. Not to worry, though, because the audience of your industry's top influencers is hanging on every word, every verbal tic, every stumble as the words on the page seem to get more distant every second. It's a flop-sweat-inducing nightmare, but it's easily avoidable with a little fore-sight.

You've spent many hours thinking about what to say, research-ing the factual foundation to support your thesis, and designing the best way to pull it all together. The next step is to present the material in a way that makes it *easy for you to deliver*. Ideally you will have learned the speech and can deliver it without notes. That way you can focus on working the audience, dazzling them with your command of the subject, charming them to your side. What you're saying is so much a part of what you believe, what you stand for, what you are, that you need no reminders, no notes, no script.

Yeah, right. Like you have the time for that. Face facts—in most cases, you're going to have to read the speech. So the next best thing is to make sure you can easily see what's written on the page, no matter what lighting conditions you're forced to work under. You have to be able to glance down, take in a good chunk of words, then look at the audience as you speak.

That's why it's best to bump up the size of the type on your copy. I'm partial to 16- or 18-point. And I like to boldface the type to supercharge the contrast with the blank white page, so that words and phrases are easy to pick up at a glance. It also helps to double-space the text and increase the size of the margins—top, bottom, left, and right. You want lots of white space on each page to highlight the words.

It's also essential to make sure that no sentence or paragraph runs over from one page to the next. There should be a period at the end of each page of the delivery text. That may mean you'll get only one paragraph on a page, with a huge amount of white space at the bottom. That's as it should be, for a couple of rea-sons. First, your text will not be stapled together, will it? No, it won't. So to go from one page to the next, you will physically move the top page off the one you're going to. This will momentarily distract you from what you're saying. And it's much better to have that distraction happen when you're taking a breath for the next sentence than in the middle of a beautifully expressed moment of wisdom.

Second, you want most of your text printed on the top half of the page, with lots of empty space at the bottom to make it easier for you to keep the audience in the game. Again, it's a subtle difference, but think about it. As you read to the bottom of a full page of text, your chin will naturally drop to maintain the angle your eyes have on the page. And when your chin drops to the page, you're not looking at the audience. Yet one of the keys to being memorable is keeping the audience in your sights. So you develop this look-and-dip motion, like one of those toy birds that constantly dips its beak into the glass of water. It's most distracting.

But if you're consulting just the top half of your page, it's easier to move back and forth between the text and your audience. Often it requires just a dip of the eyes—the chin stays in place. And the effect is that you are spending most of your time looking where you should be looking—at the audience.

As for the type itself, here are a couple of points. First, many people use a sans serif type in their word processing. I don't know why—maybe because they think it looks more modern than other typefaces. Trouble is, serif type is easier to read than sans serif. Those little tails at the ends of the letters actually help the eye move from letter to letter, from word to word. Don't believe me? Think about the books and newspapers you read. Is the body type serif or san? In most cases it's serif. And these are publications that depend on their readability to stay in business, to make money. The same point comes to my mind when I see a speech text prepared in all uppercase letters. This is a holdover from ancient history, like twenty years ago when word processors were not ubiquitous and secretaries slaved over electric typewriters. Most of these typewriters were limited in the fonts and type sizes they could deliver. So, to make the type bigger for the bosses, the secretaries typed the speech text in all caps. Trouble is, no one ever reads type in all caps in the normal course of business, except maybe telegraph operators. And when's the last time you received a telegram?

Virtually all the type you see, outside of advertising headlines and book titles, is set in upper and lower case, and there's a reason for it. Uppercase letters are not random, at least in modern English. They denote specific things: the start of a sentence, a proper name, a title. They connote importance. Thus, they give the reader subtle clues above and beyond the words on the page. They ease the process of reading and the act of comprehension. But when everything is written in upper case, those clues are lost, and the ease of reading is hobbled. It may be only a slight handicap, but why accept any impediment when you're trying to be memorable, especially one that is so easy to avoid?

Lots of white space also has one other big advantage. It gives you plenty of room to mark up the text with your own signposts and stage directions. The best speakers I know go over the delivery copy of a speech with pen in hand and their own shorthand in their heads. They double underline words they really want to hit hard. They put broad, unmistakable vertical strokes where they want to pause or to separate long phrases. They write marginalia to remind them to gesture, or to move away from the podium, even take a dramatic drink of water.

In marking the copy in this way, they not only make it easier to be stumble-free in their delivery, but they also spend more time with the speech. That enables them to become ever more familiar with the content and more cognizant of the way the speech sounds, the inherent rhythms of the prose. They are, in effect, listening to themselves deliver the speech, even if only in their heads, trying out the pace, finding the passion. It's an essential step in delivering the dynamism they're going for.

Managing the Text

I've had some executives object to guidelines such as described in the previous section. That's because texts with big type and lots of white space tend to be prodigiously long. A twenty-minute speech can run to forty pages of type. For a thirty-minute speech, you're getting close to sixty pages, which can seem like a daunting prospect. But think about how good you'll feel about the momentum in turning pages so frequently. It's like the difference between driving in the United States, where distances are measured in miles, and in Canada or Europe, where kilometers are the yardstick, so to speak. When you can click off 100 kilometers in an hour, it just seems like you're getting there faster than at 60 mph.

You also have to be able to manage the manuscript so that you're not shuffling papers, trying to find your place after you've wandered off in an extended ad lib. Rule number one, therefore, is to number your pages. If a gust of wind should send your speech notes flying, you can easily get things in the right order again.

A useful tool is the speech box, not to be confused with a voice box. This is similar to a portfolio case, only with rigid cardboard sides. It's just slightly larger in length and width than the paper you print your text on and about half an inch deep. It opens to lie flat on the podium, but its sides act like the fiddles on the countertops of a boat—they keep the pages from slipping around. At the podium, the speaker arranges the text on the right side of the box and, as he or she finishes each page, slides the finished page over to the left. It's an easy, smooth, and mostly transparent movement. The pages stay in order, and the speaker focuses on what's really important—the delivery.

One word of caution on speech boxes, however. Many lecterns, while stylish, are not designed to accommodate a speech box. They seem to have a space for paper that is exactly 8½-by-11-inch, with no margin for anything else. So make sure a speech box will fit on the podium *before* you get up there to speak. If it won't, see if the organizers will change the lectern. Remember, it's not them up there—it's you. You have to be comfortable, and it's the organizers' job to help you. If you give them enough time, they should be able to accommodate your reasonable request.

Trials of the Teleprompter

There is sometimes an alternative to delivering the speech from memory and reading it from a printed page. This is the teleprompter, and it is becoming more and more common, especially at large and important events. But like any technology, the teleprompter is a two-edged sword, offering both great support and also some risks.

On the side of virtue, the teleprompter can free you from the tyranny of the lectern, although oftentimes you'll see speakers riveted to one spot as they read from a screen. But if the venue allows it, the teleprompter can enable you to wander the stage. Just that very movement adds a dynamism that can wake up an audience.

There are some who argue that a speaker should not be all over the place, that it's distracting to see someone striding from stage left to stage right, then popping back again. I say poppycock. Speaking is theater, and theater is using the space available in the most intelligent way. It means moving right up front and center to break the invisible barrier between you and the audience for the most important sections of your talk. It means using your body and its position on stage as a prop. "On the one hand," you say as you stand stage left, "we have this set of ideas." Then, "on the other," you say as you move to stage right, "there are those who believe this. . . . The truth," you conclude moving to center front, "is, as always, somewhere in between."

With a teleprompter you're never without the script, for it's right in front of you. But you make your point in words and motion. And it seems to be effortless. Even if you're pinned on the podium behind a lectern, the teleprompter can let you read the script and keep your eye on the audience at the same time. A speaker who has had extensive training on a teleprompter can make it seem as if he or she is not reading at all, merely talking in this elegant, measured prose. It's a great tool and can be very effective.

Trouble is, there are a lot of dependencies surrounding the teleprompter, not all of which are within your control. First is the kind of teleprompter you have available. The transparent screens that politicians habitually use are the best. They are next to invisible from the audience's point of view. They hang virtually at the eye level of the speaker so he or she can appear to be looking straight out, even as he or she reads. But these are not always on offer. Oftentimes you'll get what looks like big old black and white television sets mounted on the floor. Oh yes, there are a lot of them, so you'll be able to wander all over the stage and see what's what. Of course, it will take a little practice to be able to switch from one monitor to the next as you move, but it's no big deal. Except that having the prompters on the floor is like having your entire text printed at the bottom of the page. It directs your eye, and therefore your chin and your whole face, down and away from eye contact with the audience—the drinking bird syndrome again. It's not a fatal problem, but not the optimum either, and perhaps within your power to have changed, if you find out early enough and work closely with the organizers to get it right, to your specifications.

The second issue with teleprompters is a technical one. Electrical stuff malfunctions—don't ask me why. And quite often, don't ask the techies why. The problem is, unlike with paper, when the teleprompter screen goes blank, you're stuck until someone fixes it. That takes time, and time is something you don't have when you're in the middle of your keynote speech. Murphy and his Law do happen. What's critical is to have a plan B for when he does show up. So, have a backup typewritten copy of your speech. As far as prevention, I advise a full walk-through of the teleprompter before the audience shows up. At least then you'll know that at a certain point in time, the system works. It might still blow a fuse, or the computer could crash at a critical moment, but that's the risk—and that's when you turn to plan B. Make a joke about putting a man on the moon but can't guarantee a working teleprompter, then pull out your speech box, go to the podium, and carry on.

The other risk with teleprompters is a decidedly human one. The speed at which the text scrolls up or down the screen depends on the operator of the prompter. These people are skilled, but they're not mind readers. After a brief rehearsal—before the audience shows up, of course—they can pretty much adapt the speed of the scroll to your pace in the prepared text. But they'll have trouble if you habitually leave the text for some witty anecdote or insightful aside, then paraphrase a couple of paragraphs to get back to the beaten path. This is not to say your spontaneity is a bad thing. Very few scripts cannot be improved upon on the spur of the moment. Rather, it is that by editing on the fly, you increase the risk that the prompter operator will not be able to follow the changes, and everybody will lose their place in the proceedings. You do not want to be in the embarrassing position of using hand gestures to try to get the prompter operator back on track where you think the speech should be.

Suffice to say, then, that you should be working closely with the teleprompter operator to rehearse the speech. He or she should know the general area where you may leave the text. And it's not a bad idea to mark his or her text and yours with milestones, so that if disaster strikes and you both get out of synch, you can get back on track with a quick reference to a specific point where the story picks up again.

Practice, Practice, Practice

In the room, on the day, what you say has only as much impact as how you say it. People respond to you as a person: what you're wearing, your hairstyle, your body language, the timbre of your voice, the pitch and pace of your delivery, your comfort level in the spotlight. All these are critically important in establishing the human connection between the podium and the peanut gallery. Yet 99 percent of the effort in preparing most corporate speeches goes into the "what." The "how" often involves a hurried read-through on the plane or in the cab on the way to the venue. And much of that is spent scribbling in last-minute edits in the margins of the text that, more often than not, has been finalized only the night before.

It never fails to amaze me how often, at the eleventh hour, senior executives make changes—sometimes substantive but more often not—to what they're going to say; they even make changes as they walk up to the podium. It's one thing to improvise, but quite another to fiddle with material that should have already been thoroughly vetted. For it means you'll be working new material into the act in the worst possible place—in front of a critical audience, with no safety net in case you choose the wrong word, or place the em-PHA-sis on the wrong syl-LA-ble.

The fact is that your connection with the audience, your key to being memorable, is likely to rest primarily on your performance, not the logical force of your reasoning on paper. And the only way to hone that performance is to practice performing.

Rehearse Out Loud—Several Times

The objective of any rehearsal is to know your material so well that, on the day of the performance, you can forget about everything but performing. You know the script. You recognize words and phrases. There are no surprises lurking in the midst of a long paragraph. You don't have to worry if you're running over time because you've spent some time making sure your speech fits the minutes you have been allotted. Nor do you have to concern yourself with where to raise your hands, or slow your pace, or pause. You've figured it all out. And even without memorizing the text, you're familiar enough with it that you can focus on connecting with the audience. In fact, the rehearsal is among the most important components of delivering a memorable speech. Listen to the words of Michael Caine, the British movie actor: "Rehearsal is the work; performance is the relaxation."

The rehearsal is the first time the written word becomes the spoken word. It's when your ideas are transformed into a performance, when you uncover the traps in the deathless prose spewing out of your printer. That's why you can't rehearse by simply sitting at your desk reading the text aloud, although that's better than nothing. A proper rehearsal entails standing up, ideally at a lectern with your delivery copy set up in the speech box—even more ideally with a trusted adviser watching and listening.

Everything is different when you're sitting compared to when you're standing: your body language, your pacing, even your breathing. And you want to replicate as closely as possible the conditions you'll be performing under. When you sit, even straight up as your mother taught you, your lungs cannot take in as much air as they can when you're standing. So it's tough to gauge how many words or phrases you can get in between breaths if you're behind the desk. Plus, you will tend to read much more quickly than normal—and certainly faster than you will on the podium—if you're sitting down.

Check for Tongue Twisters

To read the speech aloud, you have the involvement of the diaphragm, the lungs, the larynx, the pharynx, the lips, and perhaps the most complex mass of muscles in the body, the tongue. The anatomy of the tongue is so complex, in fact, that even today it has not been fully mapped. But our own experience tells us that this is a body part that can assume more different shapes and positions than Proteus reading the *Kama Sutra*. And it shifts from shape to shape, from position to position several dozen times for every sentence you read aloud.

It stands to reason that if your tongue can get into the right shape to pronounce a syllable, it can also get in the wrong shape and you can end up stumbling over the word. But it also stands to reason that, because the tongue is a collection of muscles, it is trainable. With exercise, it can get things right virtually all the time. And exercise means rehearsal. So find out where the tongue twisters are and change them.

To rehearse standing up is also to more closely simulate the performance you're anticipating. It's easier to envision yourself in front of the audience and go into performance mode. You'll test out how the words flow together, how your tongue will get around some of those flashy analogies. You'll find out where the land mines are: words that, even though they may be common and seemingly simple, trip you up every time. Take a sentence like this: "Spend a day with our service people, and you'll understand how crammed full our hours are." Not one difficult or unusual word in the bunch. But try to say "our hours are" three times fast. It's a difficult congruence of sounds to say, and it will be just as difficult for the listener to pick up the subtle differences in pronunciation that will let them understand your point. Clearly a rewrite is necessary, but if you hadn't practiced out loud, you might never know.

Words such as *irrelevant* often bedevil speakers, even though it is not particularly difficult to say. Same with *nuclear*, which too often, even among the most senior leaders of the free world, becomes the cringe-inducing *nu-cu-ler*. But that's only the most common problem. I had one client who always stroked out the word *significant* and replaced it with *substantial* or some other synonym. Seems that, more often than not, he stumbled over *significant,* so he avoided the trap.

The first read-through will invariably produce several stumbles, as reading out loud is something people rarely do after about the fifth grade. But that needn't result in a major rewrite. Mark the trouble areas first time out; they could be a difficult word, or a phrase that looks good on paper but just feels awkward when you say it. Or a trouble area could be a sentence that carries on forever, swooping in and out of subordinate clauses and adjectival phrases with dizzying speed.

Then, with the first trouble spots highlighted, go through the speech again and see which traps you're falling into again. Many will have disappeared, for you'll be just that much more familiar with the material. Those that remain demand that you make a call: Either highlight them so you're conscious of what's coming up or, better, eliminate them.

When you go through the speech again, there should be fewer misspoken words. You're getting more intimate with the material, sensing its innate pace. You'll quickly learn where the natural pauses occur—whether the pause is for a breath, a drink, or just for effect.

A stand-up rehearsal will likewise give you a good idea of the length of the speech. Some people can deliver 3,000 words in fifteen minutes. Others take twenty minutes, and still others are so stately in their pace that they can get through no more than 2,000 words in a twenty-minute allotment. Again, you want to know how long your speech will take you to deliver—you want to eliminate any worry on your mind except making that connection with the audience. And rehearsal lets you do that.

Pace Your Pitch and Vice Versa

Remember that a speech is not meditation. You don't want to strike a rhythm that has the unbroken stately feel of an endlessly repeated, one-note mantra. Nor is a speech a machine gun with constant short bursts of verbal ammunition strafing a word-weary audience. It is bits of both, and everything in between.

One thing most books about speechmaking do get right is the absolute necessity to vary one's pace, pitch, and force. *Pace* is the speed at which you speak. *Pitch* is the note on the musical scale you use, as in raising your pitch at the end of a question to indicate the interrogatory nature of the sentence. And *force* is the loudness, from the intimate stage whisper of confidants to the hellfire-and-brimstone shout of an emotionally committed speaker. These are elements that you need to rehearse.

In the world of pitch, pace, and force, as in the real world, too much of one thing is too much. The writing should give you clues and in many ways dictate the pace of your talk: longer explanatory sentences, delivered at a slower pace, when you're describing something of some complexity; short, staccato sentence fragments when you're driving the point home. Similarly, force will be a function of the writing. It's tough to yell a long sentence—and ineffective, too. But a short, sharp declaration? Different story. "I have a dream," indeed. That you can shout from the rooftops.

Here, the rehearsal is essential. That's the place to try out different treatments of the same words, to see how it sounds to raise the fervor in your voice as you reach the apex of your argument. to see how it feels if you actually can carry off the emotion.

Some do it better than others—and if you don't do it well, it's better not to try it than to force it. But you have to know that because you can make the call.

Truth be told, most speakers you see today give pitch, pace, and force only cursory attention. The age of inflammatory oratory is pretty much gone, as showing emotion, if not conviction, seems to have gone out of fashion. So you may want to keep it simple, which is a start. Vary the length of your sentences. Throw in the odd rhetorical question. Pause after a particularly difficult or complex section. Whatever you feel comfortable with.

Just remember how it felt to be a student on a hot June afternoon with your bologna sandwich lunch digesting away, and the teacher droning on lugubriously about the Louisiana Purchase or

Euclidean geometry or the meaning of the river in *Huck Finn*, her words a never-ending stream of undifferentiated soporific sounds. Oh yes, we all know what it's like to be on the receiving end. So now it's our job not to inflict that trial on our audiences. For here, today, the stakes may well be much higher.

Practice Your Ad-Libs

One way to change the pace and reinvigorate the audience is to step away from the text of your speech for a minute or two and actually talk to them. Ad-lib on something that has just crossed your mind.

What a concept: Actually talk to people. It's a great device, in theory. It can strengthen your connection with the audience because normally, in your little sidebar, you'll be exploring something of immediate interest—something you saw on the way to the venue, a headline in the paper that morning, a good line you heard in the foyer on your way in. It shows you're not just some automaton up there reading a canned script, at least not totally.

But ad-libbing is a learned skill. You can pay big bucks to improvisational comedy troupes to teach you the basics of coming up with something off the top of your head. And the people you see who are the best at it—most often comedians or politicians—have learned it in the heat of repeated battles as they dueled with hecklers. No question, great movies have been made that have been entirely scriptless. *Waiting for Guffman* and Christopher Guest's other "mockumentaries" come to mind. The actors were given an idea, a situation, and then left to work out the actual words on their own. The difference is, of course, that if something they tried didn't work, it went onto the cutting-room floor, and they went on to the next take. There are no mulligans at the podium.

Most speakers don't have that kind of luxury, either for do-overs or to get so much practice at being forced to think on their feet in front of a judgmental crowd. So I'm an advocate of planning your ad-libs very carefully, which makes them more of a planned lib rather than an ad-lib, but only you need to know that.

One of the big risks of an unplanned ad-lib is that it could derail you. Ask a certain erstwhile presidential candidate who went off script for a bit after losing in Iowa. You can get so involved, especially if it's a good anecdote, that you forget where you were in the text. Or the story you tell makes the point your text would make about two pages ahead, so when you get there in the text you realize you've already made the point, and probably in a more interesting way. And the audience will notice, too.

Another risk is that the story will be just slightly off topic—it seemed to be appropriate when you started, but it kind of petered out as you got further into it. Seemed like a good idea at the time, but there's no graceful way to get out of it. Time to pause, regroup, and plunge back into what you prepared. But an ad-lib that gets away from you can also set you worrying about other things that you shouldn't be worrying about in the midst of the talk. Things like the running time of the speech. If you go off script for what seems like a long time, you'll have a tendency to rush through the rest of the talk in order to finish on time. And the material you have so carefully crafted at the back end of the talk suffers for a moment's spontaneous indulgence.

So unless you're really experienced, avoid spur-of-the-moment verbal moves on stage. There's no net. Plan those ad-libs, and then rehearse them before you try them out on the audience.

Video Coaching

Many speech coaches use videotape to help the rehearsal process. There is good and bad in this approach. On the plus side, the tape doesn't lie, in that you can see how you look in general, how well you keep eye contact with the audience, how comfortable—or stiff—you and your gestures appear. You can hear where your articulation fails, where you rush and where you drag.

On the negative side, especially for people who don't do a lot of speaking, or rarely appear on tape, seeing yourself on the tube can be a confidence killer. To look at yourself stumbling around, even in the relative safety of a rehearsal studio, is unnerving at least. All your faults seem magnified. And the tape does lie—it can add ten pounds, true, but it can also flatten any emotion or humanity in the performance. It is a cool medium in which it is difficult to come off as warm and engaging. Taken together, those factors can lead to a real debilitating obsession with your vulnerabilities rather than a focus on your more dominant strengths.

It's like that experience many of us have when we ride bikes. If we're going down a path and there's a single rock in the middle of the path, where do we focus? On the rock. There's plenty of room on either side to go safely around, but we become fixated on the negative, and a collision—or at least a close call—looms. Same with a small water hazard 50 yards in front of the tee on the fourteenth hole. With no water there, we could hit the golf ball 250 yards down the fairway, no problem. With the water, it's a screaming meemie into the drink.

On balance, I favor the judicious use of training tapes, but always, always leavened with significant concentration on the positive aspects of the performance. Focus on the space around the rock, not on the rock. And go break a leg.

Key Points

- Number the pages.

- Have your delivery copy printed out in at least 16-point, bold-face type so it can be seen in almost any light condition.

- Use serif type and upper and lower case.

- Try a speech box.

- Make your mark. Develop your own shorthand editing marks to underscore important words, separate long phrases, or prompt an ad-lib.

- Practice your pauses, using them for dramatic effect or just to catch your breath.

- Vary the pitch of your voice and the pace of your reading.

- Exploit the strengths of a teleprompter. Prepare for its vulnerabilities.

- Rehearse until you can forget the details and focus on the connection with the audience.

Stand and Deliver

The time has come. It's D-day. Time to deliver. If it's a big speech, you've probably had a restless night. The adrenalin is pumping as your arrive at the venue. Now it's all about confidence—confidence that all the planning and thought that went into the content was on track; confidence that your run-throughs have made you thoroughly familiar with the material. Now it's just between you and the audience—and making that all-important connection.

Advance the Room

You often hear people, especially businesspeople and high-performance athletes and performers, talk about pushing themselves to get out of their comfort zone—that by doing so, they learn new skills and drive themselves to higher levels of success. It's a powerful idea, and not a bad model to follow for a successful life. But it doesn't work on the podium, not in front of an audience.

Everything you've done in preparing the speech up till now has been to ensure that you are well within your comfort zone in terms of the content, the audience, the timing, and everything else. You want your time on that dais to be as familiar to you as

211

possible. You want to focus on performing for and connecting with the audience, not worrying about whether it's the right time to announce this or that policy. So we get to another crucial but often underestimated commandment in the speechmaking process: Know the venue.

You have to know where you're speaking well enough that you can forget about it, remain in your physical comfort zone, zeroed in on how you're stimulating the audience. And to know it is to be there. You have to go to the venue before the event and check things out. It's called "advancing the room."

Often, this task is delegated to a subordinate. That's okay. If your flunky knows you well, knows your likes and dislikes, he or she can probably do a pretty good job of making sure most things are in place. Glass of water? *Check.* Slides in order? *Check.* Speech box fits on the lectern? *Check.*

But that's not the same as doing the checking yourself—and being thorough about it. When you rise to speak, you should feel as if you're in the meeting room where you have your weekly sessions with your team. Better still, as if you're in your living room. You must feel comfortable, so you can forget your surroundings.

There are a hundred details to check. Where do I sit before being called up to speak? How many steps up to the stage? (In the dark, it's easy to stumble.) Where is the water? Is the microphone too high or low? How do I adjust it? Does it work? Can I get a lapel mike if I prefer to wander around? Can people see me over this massive lectern? What's the possibility of getting something smaller? Or with my company's logo on it? Does my speech box fit on the lectern? Does the lectern light work? Is there a backup bulb? What's the layout of the stage, or riser? How much room do I have to move about if I wish to? How big a drop is it if I get too near the edge?

Have the lighting crew there for your walk-through so you can be sure any spotlights they plan to use don't blind you from seeing your text or interfere with your eye-to-eye connection with the audience. Check the sound system, not only to make sure it's working, without the screech of feedback, but also so you can hear what you sound like over the speakers. It's often odd to hear your own voice amplified, and the sound changes from room to room. Check it out so there are no surprises.

If you insist on using slides, run through them a couple of times, checking for proper order and, just as important, the pace of change from slide to slide. It will help calm your nerves if you know beforehand that the slides take slightly longer to switch from one to the other. Find out as well what method is being used to change the slides. Often, it's direct from a laptop on the lectern. Just make sure you can find the advance button easily, for lighting can obscure it. And make sure you know how to go back a slide, in case someone asks a question or you want to recap a point.

Other times, the button you push on the lectern sends a signal to a technician backstage, who then pushes a button to change a slide. Obviously, this takes longer than doing it directly yourself, even if the technician is paying close attention. Most times they are, but the delay can be unnerving if you're not ready for it. It doesn't hurt, either, to preview the slides from the back of the room. If you can't read them, the audience won't be able to. So it's time for some last-minute edits.

If you're using a teleprompter, run through it with the operator so he or she can gauge your pace, so you can coordinate your efforts. The goal is to create the illusion that all those pearls of wisdom are dripping from your tongue spontaneously.

You also want to know about cameras, video and other. Sometimes, you may want to make your key point looking directly into the camera, for the full delectation of future generations. More often, you want to know if the organizers have hired a still photographer. Try as they might, these shutterbugs can't help but be more intrusive than videographers, who are generally stationary. Still photographers often have to use flash, which can startle you if you're not expecting it. They'll move around a lot—now in front of you, then at the back of the room, then all of a sudden behind you on the podium, shooting over your shoulder to capture the drama of the speaker and the rapt faces of the audience. All good stuff, but you have to know beforehand if it might happen because it can be unnerving if it comes out of the blue.

All this personal checking takes time, but it's crucial to make sure you're able to forget the logistics so you can be comfortable. It's the old swimming duck theory. You paddle like hell underwater so that you look serene, confident, and wise on top. The other benefit of advancing the room yourself is that it puts you in situ early. It presents you with the opportunity to schmooze with the organizers and the early arrivals. You can listen to what's on their minds. You can get comfortable with the issues they're thinking about, their personalities. You can pick up a local reference or a topical anecdote. You can soften them up by giving them a sneak peek at your thinking (which is not to say you want to scoop yourself). You can even get an early start on picking out one or two of your visual anchors—the individuals you'll connect with during the speech. All of this serves to break down the barrier between you and the audience, or at least poke holes in it so that when you eventually do stand up to speak, you not only feel comfortable in the space but also have some higher level of acquaintance with the people in the room. A better chance to connect.

Create Your Role

If each of us is merely a player in a world that is all stage, giving a speech should be just another role, right? Clearly, for most people that is wrong. It is an almost primordial fear of the vast majority of us, up there with fear of dying or of having to watch Paris Hilton do anything.

That's why I cringe a bit when I hear presentation coaches tell nervous clients that they "just have to be themselves" when giving a speech. They mean well. "Stay within your comfort zone" is the hidden message, and it's a good one. And, thinks the client, "if I don't have to try to put on a show, it'll be easier. Heck, I'm myself 24/7. I know how to do that."

One trouble with that approach is that it can fool people into thinking they don't have to do anything different, whether they're rehashing the weather over the watercooler or facing the crowd at the convention center. Very few people have a self that is charismatic enough or big enough to make an impact in front of a room of 500 strangers, even friends. That twinkle in your eye, the way you raise your eyebrow, those funny little asides you mumble to your colleague in the middle of the meeting—none of those will work for you on the podium. The room is just too big.

It's akin to an actor who works both in film and in theater. On film, actors can do a lot with a little—a whisper here, a faint moue of the lips there, a narrowing of the eyes. When your face on screen is two stories tall, it doesn't take much to convey what's going on above and beyond the script. But on stage, you have paying customers who may be a couple of hundred feet away from you. Even portraying the same part, the theater actor knows everything has to be exaggerated in order to reach the back rows. It's a different medium.

It's the same when you're giving a speech. You may deliver fifty boardroom presentations a year. But some of the tricks you learn there will be ineffective in a large room. This is not to say you have to find a whole new "you" when you hit the dais, for you must be you. Only, as they say in the fast-food business, you have to "super-size" it. That shouldn't faze you, though. For the reality is, we all play different roles every day, and often many times during the day. At times, we'll be the confessor, listening to a colleague's woes and giving personal feedback—a fairly intimate role. Other times, we'll be the brash competitor, intent on scoring points in a meeting. Or we'll be the supplicant trying to make the sale. Or the entertainer at the bar after work. Or the authoritarian, laying down the law when the kids come home late. Or, late at night, admit it, we are the child again, curled up in a fetal position in bed, seeking solace from the vagaries of the adult world.

Speechmaker is simply another role you adopt. It's one part subject matter expert, and one part star, erudite, witty, compelling. Remember, you have your words. But you also have you: yourself as actor; your body as prop. And you get to design that prop, define the character that you will portray. Then you must stay in character.

You may talk with your hands a lot. Don't listen to coaches who tell you to keep your hands firmly by your sides. They frequently suggest that if you have your hands flailing all over the place, you'll distract the audience as you look like you're doing some sort of chicken dance. This advice is from the same people who encourage you to use flashy slides and videos, as if those gimmicks-cum-crutches aren't even more of a distraction. No, if talking with your hands is part of you, use it. But make sure it's big enough to be seen from every part of the room. You don't want to have the first three enraptured rows, people who can see everything you're doing, distracted by the restless back of the house.

If standing ramrod straight is more your style, that's fine, too, for it helps define your brand. That might not be the best thing for the CEO of a snowboard company to do, though, since it transmits a message of authority and discipline that is not appealing to the target market. I've often had coaches despair of people who grip the lectern as if it were a life ring from the *Titanic*. Or worse, lounged on it. For the grippers, I say grip away. It's not distracting, and if it helps you remain in your comfort zone, do it. For the loungers, it depends on the audience. Lounging sends a very informal, laid-back message—not, perhaps, something to do in front of bankers. But snowboarders, why not?

There are a number of critically important things to remember. First, whatever you do with your body during the speech—walk around, stand up straight, lounge around, even sit on the front edge of the table—make the action big enough that it can be seen from anywhere in the room.

Second, make sure it's authentic. If you never talk with your hands in normal conversation, don't try it in a speech. We've all seen examples in which an adviser has somehow gotten to a speaker, when it's quite obvious the stage direction is "raise your right hand here" or "hold up three fingers." Unless it's part of your ordinary modus operandi, politely thank your adviser and keep your hands in your pockets or wherever.

Third, about those hands in your pocket. Most coaches I know will say "Never." It's impolite; it's slovenly; it just looks bad. But consider this. Maybe talking to jes' folks with your hands in the front pockets of your jeans is, aw shucks, who you are. It may be a role you've adopted in your life to disarm and charm, even to fool people into thinking you may not be quite as sharp as that Brooks Brothers suit over there. More fool them, for if it's authentic to you and the personal brand attributes you've identified as important, then why not? It says, "Howdy, I'm an average Joe. Not gonna preach at ya, not gonna snow ya with a lot of big words and purty pictures. Just wanna have a little jaw 'n' see if we might could get to know each other a little better. What d'y'all say?" If that's the character you choose to play, so be it.

Remember, too, that the stage demands some dynamism,

which is sorely absent from most speeches you'll see. In the theater, during long bits of dialogue, or even in a soliloquy, it's unusual for the actors to stay in place for long. They use the space available, in three dimensions. A classical Shakespearean theater-in-the-round, for example, has entrances all over the place—stage left, right, and center, plus balconies above and trapdoors in the floor. Actors move as they speak, not just from side to side but also up and down, sometimes sitting, sometimes standing, or sometimes lying down (particularly at the end of any Shakespearean tragedy, when almost everyone has been killed off).

You have the same opportunities in your performance. You can stand, then sit, on a stool or a table's edge (just check beforehand that the table will take your weight). You can walk around, forward to the lip of the stage and back, to the lectern. Left, then right, then center. It's about commanding—not demanding—attention and giving something more to the audience than a talking head barely visible behind a lectern.

That's not always possible, of course. Many events tie you down to a stationary mike at the center of a fifty-foot-long head table. But movement is something to think about as you negotiate with the organizers, and something to rehearse as you develop the material, and again on-site as you do a run-through in preparation for speaking. Even if you are tied down, you still have things you can do. You can change the position of your hands. After standing straight up for a while, you can pointedly lean out over the lectern to emphasize a point. You can pause to take off your jacket. Point to the audience. If it fits what you're saying, and who you are or at least the role you're portraying, do it. And don't lose a minute's sleep over the people who worry that by loosening your tie you'll somehow impair the dignity of the proceedings and the power of your brand. Quite the opposite. Of course, I'm not talking about pulling a Janet Jackson halftime show stunt—

that was a bust on so many levels. But rather, I'm talking about using your physical presence to reinforce your cerebral gymnastics and enable you and your brand to stand out.

Silence Is Golden

A lot of macho management books tell us that taking no action is, in itself, an action. The implication, in this age of speed and "go for it" and the other hyped-up slogans that assault us daily, is that any action, almost regardless of consequences, is better than none. Let's leave aside for the moment the fact that many people—say, for instance, General Custer's men—might take exception to that damn-the-torpedoes advice. Instead, let's focus on how that idea operates within the context of giving a speech.

It's pretty simple, really. There seems to be this feeling among most speakers that they must fill the entire twenty minutes with words. Just keep talking; don't even pause more than a half second to take in enough oxygen to move on to your next golden phrase. Whatever happens, say something, anything, as long as you don't pause.

Is it because you're in a rush to get it all over with, to get off the rostrum in as little time as possible? Is it because you think a pause betrays some sort of nervousness? Or uncertainty as to where to go next? Is it because you're afraid the audience will fear for your health and well-being if you appear to be, even momentarily, out of control? Maybe a little bit of all of those. But wait, just a minute—literally.

Let's remember that you're not on the radio or a television talk show where dead air costs money and people blurt out the first thing that comes to mind just to cover silence. Where you are is on stage, with the spotlight on you for a period of time that can be as elastic as you want, as long as you can hold the attention of the audience. And silence is a powerful tool for grabbing people by the ears and making them pay attention.

Consider this: I can read the script for *Romeo and Juliet* in less than ninety minutes, but when I see it on stage, I have to allow three hours plus an intermission. What makes up the other ninety minutes? Well, there are a couple of sword fights, granted, and some assorted running around, even a bit of kissing. But a surprising amount of the time is taken up with silence—silence that is used to communicate the widest range of human emotions. There is the silence that carries the angst-ridden longing of star-crossed teenagers in love. There is the silence of the enormity of death—and supposed death. And that happens several times, as it turns out, with the lovers dead and the feuding families recognizing, in their solemn pauses of the final scene, the folly of their familial pride.

Tastes a bit less classical? Take Meg Ryan's famous fake-orgasm scene in the film *When Harry Met Sally*. Once she finishes her little act, there is an extended silence while the camera pans from her face, filled with I-told-you-so pride, to Billy Crystal's mix of horror and embarrassment, and then to the other diners who are, to varying degrees, shocked, amused, even turned on. All in silence.

Now let's leave aside the perhaps apocryphal story that director Rob Reiner had to teach Meg how to do the scene. And let's understand that no one is suggesting it's a good idea to fake an orgasm at the podium, or even have a real one, although no doubt either would catch someone's attention. But a well-timed pause can do a number of things.

First, it can put a bold underline on a point you've just made. ". . . and with that single, and singular initiative, we turned things around." [Long pause.] "And we have only the commitment of our customer service team to thank . . ."

Or it can set the table for a blockbuster idea: "Frankly, the street was skeptical that our industry could deliver after the meltdown of the first two years of this century. And were they right?" [Very long pause.] "Well, I can't speak for the industry, but I can tell you, as I told the analysts last week, we did deliver . . . in spades." A little silence. A lot of drama added to the delivery.

A pause engages the audience, even if it's not at a dramatic moment. For those who have dozed off, it signals a break in the action and an opportunity to jump back in, to start fresh. In that sense, a pause is another way to vary the pace of delivery, just like making sure you have some short sentences sprinkled in among the long ones. Even some sentence fragments. The human voice, especially when applied to serious subjects, can induce sleep more quickly than the soporific drone of a bumblebee on a hot July afternoon. So anything you can do to change the pace, not to mention the pitch, is one more thing in your favor.

Now, for the vast majority of audience members who are paying attention, a pause has a number of other functions: It provides a breather, a moment for reflection on what you've said before, a chance to internalize or to carry on their own inner dialogue with what you're saying. It can also, if it appears you're not reading a script, send a signal that you are thinking things through as you speak, thus creating a compelling sense of dynamism in the room.

One well-known senior political correspondent for a national television network used his pauses this way. After interviewing the usual talking heads, he would stand up in front of the camera with the lights of the legislature as his backdrop. After talking directly into the camera for twenty seconds or so, he would invariably lower his eyes and stop talking, as if giving serious thought to his next words, even though they were well prepared and rehearsed in advance. Lifting his eyes to the camera again, he would finish his spiel, leaving us all with the impression of his wisdom in the face of such momentous events.

It was pure theater, of course. He knew exactly what he was going to say next. But it was a very effective tool of engagement, until he went too far and used it every night. Moderation was not in his vocabulary. His pause, once an endearing trademark, turned into a much-mocked physical cliché, overwhelming his words and undermining his credibility.

Finally, a pause can serve you very well in the most practical of ways: to give you time to catch your breath, to get over rising nerves, even to take a drink. Many speakers I know say they start out speeches fine but after a couple of minutes, when the initial adrenaline rush has subsided, they feel an overwhelming stage fright come upon them. They can feel their voice begin to tremble. The audience blurs and the lights on the stage seem to burn more brightly, as if some tech person has put star filters on them.

What better time to pause, to take several deep breaths as inconspicuously as possible, thanks to the glass of water you can hold up to your lips, to remember that not one person in the audience wants to see you fail—that, in fact, they all want to hear what you're so well known for? As some soda pop company once said, "It's the pause that refreshes," in every sense of the word.

In fact, use silence to establish control early—right from the moment you set up behind the lectern. You may want to immediately thank the person who introduced you; that's only polite. But then, stand still and calm and silent for five, even ten seconds. Establish eye contact around the room. But say nothing.

This not only allows the audience to settle down, to get through their initial thoughts about you. It also heightens the air of expectancy as your audience edges toward the fronts of their seats, waiting for your words to begin enlightening them. And it establishes with no uncertainty who is in control. It is you who will decide when and how to share your wisdom.

It's during this pause that many good speakers pick out the friendlies. These are the three or four people in different parts of the room who can be your special guides through the speech. People who, from the first moment you make eye contact with them, seem to exude some silent empathy. They are people whose body language and facial expressions are open: no crossed arms, no scowls, no yawns. They are people you can look at, one after the other, to gauge how the speech is going and to make sure you're regularly covering all parts of the room with your beatific countenance.

Who these friendlies are will vary wildly from speaker to speaker. And it can take a little longer than the initial pause for you to identify them. But if you can pick up on even two, it makes your job all that much easier, knowing that there are at least a couple of strangers out there who are clearly on your side.

Spontaneous Comments

In the previous chapter, I stressed the need to rehearse your ad-libs along with the rest of your speech. That's not to say you shouldn't strive to be topical, even spontaneous during your performance. But make sure whatever you say off-script gives you an entry back on-script. One way to do that is to habitually set aside five to ten quiet minutes just before you go up. That's tough to do if you're speaking right after a meal, but you can always use the bathroom excuse. The idea is to closet yourself for a few minutes to get your game face on just before they say "Play ball!" That's the time to scribble in marginal notes about the amusing— and topical—story on CNN that morning. And it's the time to make sure you don't scoop yourself by telling the story too early in the talk.

What Can Go Wrong Just Might Go Wrong

It was Robbie Burns, the Bard of Scotland, who said it most famously: "The best laid schemes o' mice and men / Gang oft a-gley." Say wha? That's why we needed the apocryphal Irishman Murphy to say it so we could understand it, and put it into a law: What can go wrong will.

Then, of course, the other Irishman, O'Toole, the Dour, not wanting Murphy to get in the last word, piped up. "Murphy was an optimist." Whoever is doing the talking, the point is the same, and it is true. Things will go wrong, even if you've checked. Lectern lights will fail. Laptops will freeze. Your speech box will get knocked off the podium. Your water will spill all over the place. The teleprompter operator will lose his—and your—place. Is this a disaster? Or an opportunity? The choice is yours.

If you've prepared well enough, nothing should stop you. A technical foul-up, or worse, may break your stride but not break your spirit. Tom Rosshirt is a speechwriter who worked in the Clinton White House. He likes to tell the story at conferences nowadays of the time the president was to deliver a major speech that everyone had worked very hard to get just right. The story goes like this.

Bill Clinton was last on the agenda that day. As he moved to the lectern, he looked down at the notes that had been put there beforehand so he wouldn't be seen to be carrying a sheaf of paper around. He paused, rather longer than normal, close observers thought. Then he launched into what Tom called a breathtakingly erudite forty-minute speech. It was generally on the topic they'd talked about, but it didn't cover most of the points they'd labored over, or use the rhetoric they'd sweated to get down.

After the speech, the writers congratulated the Chief. "But," said one of them, "you didn't seem to use a lot of the material we worked on."

"Funny thing, that," said Clinton. "I guess the lady who spoke before me picked up my notes, too, when she left the stage. 'Cause when I got up there, there was nothing there."

Forty minutes. Closely reasoned, articulate. He had no notes, and no one noticed. That's *being prepared*. In the speechmaking world, that's as close as you're going to get to Hemingway's definition of guts: "grace under fire."

When things go wrong, you gain the opportunity to super-charge the boost your appearance is giving to your brand and that of your organization. That because people have an innate sympathy for speakers to begin with. But much more important, they have a well-documented tendency to turn on the admiration jets for anyone who gets out of a sticky situation with good grace and humor.

So be ready to turn disaster into not just sympathy but admiration for the calm, cool, and collected way you handle the situation. Take a breath. A long pause. Acknowledge the problem up front. If it can be fixed, have a back-pocket anecdote ready to stall for time. If it's not fixable, say so and carry on—only make it seem as if this were really what you would have preferred in the first place.

"Ladies and gentlemen, I am sorry. This [insert problem here] just doesn't want to go away. But that's okay, because it gives me a chance to do what I really want to do any way—talk with you, not at you."

The venue and the nature of the problem will largely determine what specific steps you can take. If it's a typical hotel dining room, smaller rather than larger, you may be able to step away from the dais and move into the middle of the room, enabling everyone to hear you no matter if the sound system has crapped out. If it's a repeat performance of the great blackout of 2003, you may be stuck—in which case you become no longer the guest speaker but the chief emergency coordinator, at least until you can hand off to your hosts. And chances are that you may even get more Brownie points for doing that than for anything you might have said in your prepared remarks.

Whatever happens, comfort yourself with this thought: "This is not brain surgery." No matter what you say or do, no one's going to die.

The Last Word

A great debate rages in the speechmaking profession today. Well, that may be a little strong. Speechwriters rarely rage about anything, even repeated dangling modifiers. Let's just say there are mixed opinions on how to end a speech.

Not the summary. For my part, I prefer a quick wrap-up. If you've done your job right, you probably don't need more than a couple of sentences to reiterate your theme and make your call to action. Others prefer a more fulsome recapitulation.

No, this debate is over the question of whether you should thank the audience. I had one instructor who was definitely in the "no" camp. "They should be thanking you for going to all that trouble." Well, yes, that's true.

On the other hand, for many people including me, saying thank you at the end of the speech is a must. For one thing, "Thank you" serves as a verbal applause sign, and goodness knows some audiences need all the clues you can give them in order to respond in an appropriate manner.

But more important, it's the polite thing to do. The people in the audience have gone to some expense and trouble to listen to your sermon. You've imposed on their time, twenty minutes or more that they'll never get back. So acknowledge their critical role in your performance.

And finally, what can it hurt?

Key Points

- Arrive early to get the lay of the land, and listen to the pretalk chitchat.

- Once onstage, be yourself—only a little bit better.

- Use your body as your prop—move around, gesture.

- Use every available bit of space to vary the visual effect.

- Have confidence to leave the script for planned ad-libs, but know where you're going and don't stay too long.

- If something goes wrong, take advantage of the situation to gain audience sympathy.

- Say "Thank you."

After the Talking's Done

When all is said and done, all is not said and done. What gets done after the speech is delivered is one of the most important aspects of creating a memorable impression and enhancing your personal brand. Yet this phase is ignored for the most part, except for some cursory e-mails of the "How'd I do?" and "You did great, Boss" variety.

There are two key ways you can benefit from some thorough follow-up. First, if you want to keep improving as a speaker, you need feedback to help you get better, in terms of both the content and your role as a performer. Second, you can take steps to spread the word beyond the audience who happened to join you in the room on that day. Let's look at both in turn.

How'd I Do?

If you want to find out how your performance went, just ask. Of course it's not as simple as that. But start with yourself. Where do you think you stumbled? At which points in the speech did you feel you were losing the audience? You can often tell, just by checking the body language and noise levels in the audience. Where did you think you were boffo? At what point did your performance match what you envisioned in your rehearsal—in your dreams?

Remember, though, that this is only a starting point. Some people are invariably too tough on themselves. Others are more lenient, to the point of laissez-faire. Either extreme—self-flagellation or -adoration—is likely not all that useful in shaping your next performance. But it's one perspective, and an important one, for no one experiences your speech quite the way you do. You have everything to gain by being brutally honest with yourself, even if it's realizing that, hey, you knocked it out of the park.

Beyond that, though, it's critical to find other trusted viewpoints. You can ask the colleagues who attended the session with you. But the frankness—and therefore the usefulness—of their answers will depend on the kind of relationship you have with them and the power differential between them and you. No one likes to be told he or she has flopped. Some executives brook little criticism from their lieutenants—after all, if they're so smart, why aren't they the boss? That said, most professional executives will have the integrity to tell you the truth, although it will almost always be cushioned in language that would do a diplomat proud. So take the praise with a grain of salt. And add a bit more spice to the mild suggestions for improvement you hear from these folks, adjusting for the level of frankness that normally holds sway in your relationship.

Then, of course, there is the audience. One gauge of your success is how many people came up to you afterwards to ask questions, make comments, exchange cards. Some of these people will no doubt be glad-handers looking to polish their own apple in the glow of your greatness. But many will be genuinely moved to introduce themselves by the cogency of your argument and the evocative nature of your performance. You can get at least anecdotal evidence of how well you did by the nature of the questions and comments they make.

It can also be useful to keep your ears open as you exit the locale, eavesdropping on unsolicited comments of audience members, one to another. In these comments often lies the truth, for there is no grandstanding here, no politics of power. That's why I often wander around the lobby after a client's speech, my ear cocked for any tidbits, good or bad, to feed back to the client and add to my own grab bag of intelligence. It's the same reason I spend as much time at a speech watching the audience as I do the speaker. I'm looking for heads nodding, in agreement or off. For clock watching or e-mail checking.

For many major events, there is also the opportunity for formal audience evaluations. Often this is put together by the organizers who will, after crunching the numbers, give you the results of what the surveyed audience made of your appearance. But I have also known cases in which the speaker's organization put together its own postspeech poll. In the absence of something done by the organizers, this is not a bad idea, as it gives you what you need most: a relatively unfiltered critique by the most important people involved in the speech—the audience.

Another technique that can be effective is to videotape the performance (often the organizers will do this as a matter of course) and then view it with a critical eye. Athletes do that all the time, breaking down their batting swing, or their break from the starting blocks, into incremental frames of exactitude. But tape is a tricky tool, and if you use it, it can really help to have on hand a professional presentation coach.

This coach is needed not only to put the screws to your performance—to point out your mannerisms or annoying idiosyncrasies, or perhaps where you kept your head down too long—but also to give positive feedback. For there is almost always a palpable difference between the speech as given in the room and as captured on tape. I have witnessed speeches that have held the audience in thrall till the last moment, when the standing ovation started. Yet on tape, the same speech seemed flat, or forced, or overwrought.

In one case, the speaker was on a real emotional high coming out of the room after a big speech that had a rousing finish, including a stirring bit where he essentially wrapped himself in the national flag. He received lots of nodding heads and ultimately a standing O. And he couldn't wait for his wife to see his performance later that evening on the local cable television station. When he came in the next day, he looked deflated. Surprised, I asked him how his wife—an unfailing booster—had liked his stellar performance. "She thought it was okay," he kind of mumbled. "And I thought so, too—it seemed better in person. On tape there was something missing."

I hadn't seen the tape, but I went in search of it and I saw what the boss and his wife had seen—a vast difference in energy between the live experience and the tape. One of the problems was that, although they had used two cameras, both were trained almost exclusively on the speaker. There were few if any cuts to the audience, in either pictures or sound. So it was as if the speaker were doing his thing in a sterile studio.

No question, the media filter of the videotape and monitor bleached out much of the humanity and dynamism of the in-room experience. And the difference in impact was huge. That's why you need a coach present when you're looking at your tapes—someone who understands that the tape is a useful tool to identify that hitch in your swing, as when you fix your tie every 30 seconds, or say "Um" with every new breath. The coach also knows that the medium of tape will more often than not flatten the dynamism of the event, and can keep you from being too self-critical based on a perspective that doesn't give the whole picture. In fact, it can be useful to schedule an annual refresher session on presentation skills. Get a coach to go over the tapes you've made during the year and pull together a reel that shows where you've fixed your tics and where you haven't. It's a pretty painless way of bringing some discipline to your performance development. For in the end, all this feedback is useless unless you do something with it. Acknowledge the advice and build improvement into your preparation for the next speech.

That is not to say you should accept all the advice willy-nilly. You cannot turn off your own discriminatory powers just because one frustrated listener fought with her partner and needed to take it out on somebody. Not all advice is good advice. And you must make the final call on what is right for you. Like everything else about your speech, you have the ultimate power because the words are coming out of your mouth.

Enlist the Messengers

A lot of the mileage you'll get from your speech is word of mouth—from your own mouth to the listeners in the room, and from their mouths to their own circles of influence once they leave the venue. "That was a great line old Goodfella had, wasn't it?" "Can you believe . . . what was it Johnson said . . . our industry sector is going to have to cut its spending by half in the next ten years—that is gonna leave a mark." Or better: "Sir, you should hear what Angela Mahoney said about the implications of the aging population on productivity. I think we'd better start doing something about it or we're going to have a lot of our pensioners struggling to make ends meet."

Apart from the "Aha!"s in the room, that's where the real return on investment comes for the work you've done putting your views on the table. A memorable talk can elevate public discourse and connect you with important thought leadership. Alas, if you're mediocre, it's likely that word of mouth will go no farther than the first level, the audience. If you're great—or awful—your name and point of view will be on everyone's lips. But it's not enough just to say the words and then hope they'll ripple through to people who weren't in the room. There are ways to keep the momentum going yourself.

It starts with inviting the messengers. In the most obvious sense, that means the media. They're paid to carry messages, and their reach is truly phenomenal, for good or bad. Clearly, major papers, news magazines, radio, and television—coming into tens of millions of homes and offices—offer extraordinarily exposure for you—and for every other person who thinks he or she has a unique perspective on the history of humanity.

If you can get the media to attend, well done. But you have to trim your sails to suit the wind, and even a light breeze—like a trade magazine article about your speech or a cable television broadcast of the tape—can blow your brand in the right direction. Clearly, the problem with the public media is that you have no control over them. But you do have some clout when it comes to what your internal media say. It never fails to amaze me how seldom executives think to send copies of their speeches to the people in charge of an organization's house organ. And they rarely if ever invite company editors and writers to the event itself. What an opportunity missed when you have a captive audience and a guaranteed friendly editorial stance! All it takes is a phone call or an e-mail, for I speak from years of experience. House communications people are always, always searching for solid, substantial stories about something other than sales results or bowling tournaments. And every employee who reads the speech is a potential ambassador for the ideas in it, and for your personal brand.

Enlisting the messengers also includes inviting or inveigling influential colleagues and friends to attend—even paying for their tickets. This accomplishes a couple of things. First, it ensures that you have at least some allies in the room—people you know agree with what you're saying and how you're saying it. That alone can help calm your nerves when you stare out into the spotlight. Just as important, it effectively enlists messengers who will be predisposed to spread the word of your brilliance to others in your organization and to anyone in their circle of acquaintance they think is appropriate. Through them, you can reach more people who should hear what you're saying but weren't able to be there.

Through these messengers you can also distribute copies of the text so that the paper no longer appears out of the blue on a desk, but comes with a little sticky note: "Thought this talk by my colleague might interest you, Dave. How about lunch next week?" Not only do you get more exposure, the exposure comes with the tacit endorsement of a person already in some relationship with the recipient: It's no longer a cold call for your words. More than that, it benefits your messenger colleague, for it gives him or her another reason to get in touch with important clients and contacts.

This is not to suggest you should be free and easy with the postdelivery distribution of the text. People are sometimes, ah, reluctant to receive unsolicited messages from people they don't know. So not every speech should go to every contact in your address book, paper or electronic. But you should give thought to who might be interested in or pleasantly surprised by your enterprise. Consider, for example, media columnists who seem never to attend anything in person, but view the world through the business end of a telephone and e-mail. What about your own executive colleagues, within your company and in your industry? Your board of directors? Key customers should almost always be getting what you produce. Again, even if they don't read the text, they at least see you're out there being a thought leader. And it gives you a good excuse to follow up in person to keep the relationship warm.

There are even publications that print nothing but speeches or speech excerpts. Most people don't read these, but speechwriters do. And that gives your ideas, your *bon mots*, a chance to be cited by other leaders. You become the expert source. Why not? All it costs is the paper, ink, and postage or the electricity to send the e-mail. Plus, if you make a habit of getting your production team to do a nice job designing and packaging the material, before you know it you'll have the makings of a book that someone may publish. At the very least, you'll be able to get someone to put some nice leather covers around your oeuvre and give it pride of place in your den. (Your kids may someday want to learn more about what you did when you disappeared from home every day.)

Amortize the Investment

Every time you get a copy of your speech into the hands of someone else, you've improved the chance that you'll actually get a return on your investment of time and resources. But just distributing the speech to broader and broader audiences is not enough.

You should think seriously about repackaging the content to provide more shelf life. The simplest way is to hand it to your Web gurus and have them post it in a format that is easy to read (and print from) on your organization's Web site. The printer-friendly version is not trivial. I can't tell you how frustrating it is to print something from a Web site only to discover, thirty pages later, that about an inch of the text on the right-hand side of the page is lopped off. I've just wasted time and paper, and I'm less disposed to bother to go back and cite the author.

With a little more effort, there are many other ways to distribute your text. The normal twenty-minute speech will be around 2,500 words, for instance. With some judicious trimming, most speeches can be brought down to the 500 to 800 words that news editors look for in op-ed pieces. Again, your media people may not be able to sell it to the editorial page editors of *The New York Times* or *The Washington Post*. But there are hundreds of other newspapers that tens of millions of people read. Those editors all have acres of white space to fill, every day. And that doesn't include editors of magazines, in particular the publications that specialize in covering your industry. They will often accept material cut down from speeches, for it enables them to feature an industry expert—you.

Nor does it include expert commentators for electronic media. Ever wonder how news networks so quickly find those retired generals and security experts to appear on camera as soon as there's a new war or terror incident? Those people are in the pool, and they got there by making their expertise known to the producers. When I ran the public relations department for one of the continent's major research universities, every year we produced a booklet of all the faculty experts and the areas in which they were qualified and willing to comment in the media. We sent this to every reporter and producer we could think of—and they used it. They knew they had trained experts within easy reach.

On the strength of having delivered a speech, you are an expert on that topic. Use that simple fact to increase your profile and build your brand. And your media people should be ready to help you.

Save Your Video Money

Back in the antediluvian period before Tim Berners-Lee gave us the Worldwide Web, I worked for a leading maker of telecommunications equipment. And when they said "leading," that wasn't just corporate bragging. This was indeed one of the top three in the world, with tens of thousands of employees in ninety countries.

It's not easy to communicate to so many people in so many places in a timely manner, but we tried. One of the ideas was to create a quarterly video newsmagazine. This was a lushly produced fifteen-minute mélange of messages from the top executives, mixed in with dynamic footage of emergency situations overcome and beauty shots of the incredible found art of new technologies. We then shipped out multiple copies of these tapes to every location in the company, where they were displayed in specially made racks in lunch rooms and employee lounges. The racks came with built-in televisions and tape players so the staff could view the tapes during their breaks. Or they could borrow the material to take home and share the excitement with their families.

Great idea, except no one watched the tapes. Local reps kept track of how often the inventory moved off the shelves. Their conclusion: not very often. And these represented weeks of work, tens of thousands of dollars in production and distribution—for nothing. Why? Here was this gee-whiz electronic technology—an innovative approach to communicating with employees—with production values equal to the best network television news shows and stories that directly affected the target audience. But in hindsight, we should have seen it coming.

First, who wants to watch company propaganda when you're on a break? Or inflict it on the family when *Jeopardy* is on? More than that, though, there are intrinsic problems with expecting people to watch a videotape they get for free. And that's why any plans you have to videotape your speech and send copies to all your friends and contact targets should be thought through twice, at least.

Second, watching a videotape of a speech takes a long time—much longer than the time it takes to read the text. With paper text, a reader's eye can scan great chunks of sentences very quickly, pulling in the highlights in a matter of a very few minutes. And there are no pauses while the speaker gathers his wits, or shuffles paper, or waits for the applause to die down. Plus, to watch a video, you have to be set up: You need the machine, the monitor, and an electrical supply. With a text, you can read it any-where—even while the mute button's on during a conference call—and easily carry it around with you, even to the breakfast table or the bathroom. No matter what the technophiles tell you, plain paper and ink is a medium that still has advantages over the most sophisticated handheld personal computing device.

In that context, a paper text of your speech has it all over a video when it comes to being easy to use. What's more, it's more respectful of your target's time. Put yourself in the place of the people you're sending your material to. Would you rather get a video that will take twenty minutes to view, not counting all the time it takes to find a machine to play it, or would you rather get a text you can read in the cab to the airport?

The same reasoning applies to streaming video on the Web. It can be tempting to send e-mails to your contacts, letting them know your most recent performance is on the Web site and pro-viding the hot link. No imposition, right? If they don't want to watch it, they don't have to. If they do, it's a bonus for you. That's all right as far as it goes, but the same reasoning applies to Web-casting as to videos. In most cases, the quality is still not even as good as a single-camera community auction on the local cable TV outlet. And it still takes time to find and to watch—more time than it takes to scan a printed text. Call me antediluvian. Call me a dinosaur. But when it comes to sending out videos of your speeches to influence people, save your money and warm up the photocopier.

Key Points

- Obtain feedback from a variety of sources—and pay attention to it.

- Enlist messengers to spread the key points.

- Distribute copies to key influencers who weren't in the room.

- Don't forget house organs.

- Repackage material for op-eds, white papers.

- Save your video money.

The Speaker's Checklist

Preacceptance

Is it the right audience?
- ☑ Number of participants
- ☑ Organizational level of participants
- ☑ Customers
- ☑ Market/regulatory influencers

Is it the right venue/format?
- ☑ Panel or keynote
- ☑ Level / quality of other speakers
- ☑ Prominence of organizing / sponsoring group
- ☑ Sponsorship opportunities
- ☑ Extent of synchronicity between organizers' wishes and your message priorities
- ☑ Better opportunities elsewhere
- ☑ Audiovisual expectations
- ☑ Media invited

Is it the right time?
- ☑ Does your organization have something to announce?
- ☑ What else is going on in the company/industry that might enable you to use this as a platform?

☑ What else is going on in the company/industry that might make you adopt a lower profile?

What is the sponsoring organizer's marketing plan?
☑ Will they fulfill their obligation to get the audience there?
☑ What plans do they have to distribute material after the conference?

Development Phase

• Book time in planner for rehearsal.

• Provide staff with heads up, as appropriate:
   ○ Communications adviser
   ○ Media relations
   ○ Issues management
   ○ Strategic planning
   ○ CorpComm VP

• Arrange for approvals, as appropriate
   ○ Communications adviser
   ○ Media relations
   ○ Issues management
   ○ Strategic planning
   ○ CorpComm VP

• Confirm a/v arrangements with organizers.
   ○ Type of microphone (lavaliere, on lectern)
   ○ Stage setup
   ○ Lighting (will it be videotaped?)
   ○ Audience seating arrangement

- Confirm room arrangements, audience size with organizers.

- Check if organizers plan a feedback mechanism.

- Consult with media relations re potential news release, scrum possibilities.

Delivery

The room itself
- ☑ Are copies of the speech properly displayed and at the right time (preferably not before the talk)?
- ☑ Are there proper signs directing people to the room?
- ☑ Do the signs acknowledge the role of my organization?
- ☑ Where will the video cameras be?
- ☑ Where will the still photographer be?
- ☑ Where will the media be sitting?
- ☑ Is there a reception room for after?

The stage/podium
- ☑ Where do I sit prior to the speech?
- ☑ How do I get up on stage?
- ☑ How many stairs?
- ☑ Is there room to move around while I'm talking?
- ☑ Can I get out from behind the lectern or head table?
- ☑ How big a drop is it from the stage or riser to the level of the audience?
- ☑ What's the seating arrangement?
- ☑ Can I wander through the audience or am I to be stationary?
- ☑ Where do I go when I'm finished?

The lectern

- ☑ How bulky is it—i.e., can more than my head and shoulders be seen?
- ☑ Does the light work?
- ☑ Will my speech box fit on it?
- ☑ Can I get my organization's logo displayed on it?
- ☑ Where does the water glass sit?
- ☑ Is there a timer?

The audiovisual support

- ☑ What will be the level of lighting when I speak?
- ☑ Will there be a spotlight, and how will it affect my view of my text and the audience?
- ☑ Do the a/v suppliers have the slides ready to go and on a backup?
- ☑ How do I change the slides, backwards or forward?
- ☑ Does the microphone work?
- ☑ Do I have a choice of a lapel mike?
- ☑ If it's a fixed mike, how do I adjust it to the right height?
- ☑ Is there a small riser for the speaker (if short)?

Postdelivery

- What is audience feedback?

- Should hard copies of the speech be sent to key stakeholders?
  - ○ Board members
  - ○ Government/regulatory
  - ○ Key customers
  - ○ Media
  - ○ Speech publications

- Should the speech be repackaged for Web site, op-ed piece, or internal publications?

APPENDIX B

Research Resources

The Internet has brought much of the world's information to your desktop with a few strokes of the keyboard and a click or two of the mouse. Every researcher will have his or her own favorite search engines, portals, and Web sites. And once you get started down a path, you will no doubt come up with your own in a matter of minutes.

I just this minute did an MSN search on the word *quotations* and got 1,430,385 hits. Who am I to suggest which are the best Web sites in that deep pool? But here are just a few general sites I do find useful:

- http://www.libraryspot.com. A portal that opens paths to dictionaries, thesauruses, advice on style and grammar, almanacs, and a variety of specialized library material, from law to medicine.

- http://www.bartleby.com. Famous as a major source of quotations, also features writing reference books including usage guides by Strunk and White, and Fowler).

- http://infoplace.com. A portal that has a huge pool of information on a wide variety of topics. Of special interest is its "This Day in History" section, plus U.S. and international statistics.

- http://historychannel.com/thisday/. A source for what happened on a particular day in history.

- http://www.datadragon.com/day/. What happened on specific dates in music history.

- http://www.quoteland.com. Just what it says—dedicated to all sorts of quotations.

- http://www.quotationspage.com and http://www.famousquotations.com. Sources for more quotations—like I said, there's a million of 'em.

- http://www.fedstats.gov. Statistical data from more than 100 U.S. federal agencies.

- http://www.govspot.com. Masses of statistics, including the CIA World Fact Book, Census Bureau, and National Archives.

- http://www.oecd.org. Home site for the Organization for Economic Co-operation and Development, this offers lots of information on international economic comparisons.

- http://www.achievement.org. Profiles, biographies, and interviews with dozens of individuals who have shaped recent domestic and international history in the arts, business, government, science, sports, and so on.

As for books on my reference shelf, many are specialized but there are a few that touch on writing and the use of language, including:

> *The Chicago Manual of Style*, 15th Edition. Chicago: University of Chicago Press, 2003.

Allan, R. E., and H. W. Fowler, editors. *Oxford Pocket Fowler's Modern English Usage*. London: Oxford University Press, 2002.

Blamires, Harry Blamires, et al. *The Penguin Guide to Plain English*. New York: Penguin Books, 2000.

Bryson, Bill. *Troublesome Words, 3*rd Edition. London: Penguin Books, 2002.

APPENDIX C

When Someone Else Will Write Your Speech

No one is better positioned to know what you want to say and how you want to say it than you. That said, many senior executives with oversubscribed timetables turn to others to prepare their remarks for everything from ribbon cuttings to industry-leading think pieces. So you have to weigh the pros and cons of make or buy.

Clearly time and expense are critical elements. Do you have the time? Can you afford to have someone else do it? Trust is another issue, because if you're not writing it yourself, you had better trust the person or people you're depending on to put words in your mouth and help you build your personal brand. In many ways, developing that trust is as time-consuming as writing the speech yourself. It takes time for any writer to get to know you, to understand not only the ideas in your head but the cadences of your speech. It takes time for a writer to know that a person says "nu-cu-lar" and that the word nuclear should therefore be avoided. Time to bring out the humanity in you that will create the audience connection. And it takes time for you to drill into the writer—and your other advisers—that you're not going to settle for good enough. That your objective is to be memorable.

Internal Writer or Freelance?

If your decision is to buy rather than write, a whole set of questions comes into play. First question: Should you get someone in the organization to do it or hire freelance?

There are advantages either way, so it's a judgment call. If you tap one of your PR people on the shoulder to be the scribe, you get someone who you expect will know not only your organization but also your industry. They'll have, as part of their everyday working mind-set, an understanding of the environment in which you work, the pain points your organization is dealing with, and the priorities you're driving in order to reach your objectives. This can save you a lot of time because you can speak with this person in the sort of internal shorthand that you use with other executives. "Yeah, we should cover the D-Slam extension program, and what's-his-name over in CS can give you the IVR story—good example of the M² Vision thing." An outside writer just might have a few time-consuming questions around those acronyms, not to mention the philosophical foundation for the vision.

In addition, an internal writer comes with a built-in higher level of trust. The person clearly has a strong commitment to your organization, having entrusted his or her career to your team, at least for now. This person is a known quantity. Chances are that you've seen something this person has written . . . and liked it. You can also check this person out with any number of colleagues, not only his or her credentialed *bona fides* but also the way this writer works and whether it fits with your expectations. And, given the hierarchical nature of most organizations, you can be more confident this person will, in the end, do as told.

It's also often easier to develop a long-term relationship with an internal colleague, someone whose office is just down the hall or who is, at least, available on the same internal e-mail server. For often the most fruitful exchanges between writer and speaker happen in brief, informal encounters. I once had an office in the middle of a long hallway. At one end of the hallway was the office of the company's chief financial officer, obviously a key player in the senior executive ranks and a close confidante of the chief executive officer. At the other end of the hallway, in the other corner office, sat the CEO. Several times a day, one or the other of them would make the trek to the other one's office. And as often as not, one or the other of them would stop for a chat at the halfway point, in my office. Sometimes they'd drop off a book, or a magazine article they'd been reading, or hadn't read but wanted to but didn't have time, so could I please have a look and tell them if there was anything good there. Other times, they'd just say, "You know, I've been thinking . . ." and we'd be into an interesting little conversation. It might not be about a specific project in the pipeline at the moment, but it was all grist for the mill. And many of the ideas tossed out in that setting surfaced later in speeches by both of them. For all three of us, it was a natural part of the speech-making process, a process that never stopped because we knew some day there would be another opportunity to sell our brand from the podium.

Using an internal writer eliminates much of the risk of hiring an outsider. And there is risk. For although there are plenty of freelance writers out there, like the field of practitioners in any other quasi profession, there are plenty who are mediocre at best. Put more charitably, there are too many who have strengths in areas that may not match your need to build your brand on the podium. Finding one who combines writing and research skills with the ability to understand your ideas and capture the way you express them is critically important. Remember, it's not the writer who's standing on the podium, it's you. So it's a search you want to complete as quickly as possible. And if there's talent in the backyard, why not use it?

The External Perspective

Given all that, why would one ever hire an outsider? There are lots of reasons, good reasons. Start with the fact that few companies can afford the luxury of a full-time speechwriter on staff. I once worked for a utility that had an entire speechwriting unit: three writers, an executive assistant/junior writer for ribbon cutting ceremonies, plus a manager. Our mandate was to write for the chairman, the president, and half a dozen senior vice-presidents. That's all. I used to limit my output to about 200 words in the morning so I'd have something to do in the afternoon. But that place was an exception. In most cases today, staff writers have many duties and obligations. Often, the only people senior enough to tackle an officer's speech are the leaders of the PR units who have a pile of other responsibilities as well.

Then consider that a speech is a unique and quite specialized form of writing. Unlike a memo, or letter, or op-ed piece, or article for the employee magazine, a speech is first and foremost an aural creature. It is made to be listened to. When I was being interviewed for my first pure speechwriting job—at the aforementioned utility—the manager of the writing unit chatted for about five minutes about the usual stuff on my résumé. Then he surprised me.

"Do you play an instrument, a musical instrument?" he asked. I couldn't figure out where he was going, so I had him repeat his question. Had he been burned by an irresponsible musician? Or was he trying to be friendly? It never occurred to me that he was asking a key question for a speechwriter.

Not being able to think of a suitably neutral response, I told the truth: "Well, a little guitar, but mostly I'm a singer, in church choirs and garage rock bands."

"Great," he said, showing me not for the last time just how astute he was and is.

Not that I got it yet. "Why do you ask?" I said in my naiveté.

"Because a speech is made to be listened to. It has to have a rhythm. It has to have quiet parts and crescendos. It has to have changes in pitch and pace, and an overall structure and shape. It has to have words that are easy to say and that are clear to be understood and appreciated by the audience. I just find that the best speechwriters I've ever worked with have also had musical training. They could write for the ear."

A speech is also a sustained soliloquy, an implied dialogue between the main actor and the audience. As such, it is quite different, in length and tone, than white paper, or a business case, or a memo. It is not every writer who can sustain 3,000 words of prose that will first connect with the audience and keep them hooked for 20 minutes. And so there are specialists. Occasionally you'll find them inside large organizations. But more often they are off on their own, exploring the speechwriting niche with a number of different organizations. The best ones bring to the table not only a facility with the language, but an ear for syntax and rhythm. Not to mention the ability to interact with people at all levels of your organization. For although the most critical contact is between writer and speaker, the writer will also have to muck about in the entrails of the organization to find the telling anecdotes and compelling evidence that support the speaker's strategic vision.

Apart from a specialist's skill, the outside writer also brings to bear a fresh and more independent eye. He or she is less likely to be inculcated with the daily dose of propaganda that floods from corporate communications vehicles. He or she is less likely to spout your organization's bizspeak—the trite phrases that cause eyes to glaze over, and speeches to be forgotten. A good freelancer will challenge what may be your organization's received wisdom, or at least the way it is articulated. He or she has the freedom to do that that an insider never has. And sometimes, even often, when the normal way of saying something is not blindly accepted but put under such scrutiny, you come up with a better way to say it.

In that way, the freelancer lives, in an intellectual sense, closer to where the audience is. He or she is, in fact, a credible proxy for the audience in most cases, having about as much invested in your organization's cause as any group of interested by not committed listeners.

Certainly it is true that this is a role internal public relations people can play. In theory at least, the best PR practitioners live in the kind of never-never land between the company and the outside world. Their role is twofold: one, to send out to that world the best that the company has to offer; and two, to reflect the opinions and beliefs of the outside world back into the organization, in the best of all worlds influencing the company's behavior so that it garners the most support possible from its various publics.

As my father used to say, PR is a lonely profession. You have to be "in" the company, but not "of" the company. You're not doing your job if you simply parrot what the mastodons tell you to say. You have to push back, to represent the audience.

Unfortunately, this part of the role of the PR practitioners is more honored in the breach than any other way. In many if not most organizations, the objective of PR is more toward the cheerleading/gladhanding end of the spectrum. Senior executives don't want to hear bad news. And they often pay people to not tell them.

So it becomes easier for an external writer, with no pension plan on the line, to ask the mischievous questions, to poke around the edges of The Truth as the company believes it to be. But that poking can be an extremely important part of coming to an articulation of a position that will, in fact, create a memorable experience for an audience. For it will contain the credibility—explicit or not—that examined beliefs embody.

But never forget that no one knows you better than you. No one has more vested in your personal brand than you. You might want some help shaping your ideas, but in the end, the words you utter will be associated with you. You must make them yours.

Finding the Right Writer

There are a couple of key things to ask any prospective freelancer. First, of course, is he or she musical? Second, there's experience, and there are a number of dimensions to this simple question.

To begin, what experience does the person have writing speeches? If he starts to pull out brochures and video scripts and published articles, stop right there. You want to see speeches. They're very different than any other type of corporate writing. Nor can you be happy with some slide presentations the person has put together. You're hiring this person for his ability to put the right words in your mouth in the right order. You don't need him to be a graphic artist.

What's more, ask to see the first draft of speeches, not the final versions. The reality is that, between what a writer initially puts down on paper and what eventually comes out of the speaker's mouth, there can be a Grand Canyon of difference. Many organizations let any number of people provide comments on first drafts. Many times the comments significantly alter the ability of the speaker to connect with the audience. Too often the final version reads like what it is: written by a committee.

By asking to see a first draft, you can assess firsthand if this person can, without input from others, set the hook in the audience, build a case, tell a story, sustain the argument, and finish on a high note. If she can't, then you should be prepared to do some hands-on managing of the speech process. But that's not why you hire a writer.

The other key thing to ask a prospective writer is to provide a list of clients. Here you're not looking for company names as much as for the specific persons for whom the writer wrote. Is he or she used to dealing with chairmen and CEOs, or is it more at the VP level? Nothing wrong with that, necessarily, but there is almost always more at stake when a CEO speaks than in the case of a more junior executive.

Knowing the specific people with whom the writer has worked also gives you an opportunity, if you wish, to get some personal insights into not only the writer's skills but also the way he works. I have known writers with long and impressive lists of clients. Some were tireless researchers who could dig up obscure content from a wide range of sources. They were presentable, easily able to hold their own in face-to-face meetings with the most senior executives. Their finished speeches looked great—punchy, full of content, on message. But their first drafts were horrendous. Twice as long as they should have been. Wandering off into interesting but not germane culs-de-sac of thought. Plus they loved to make the whole thing an interactive process—they were always on the phone, trying out ideas. To hire them was to engage in a time-consuming management process that defeated the whole purpose of getting them involved in the first place. In at least one case, I simply gave up and rewrote the speech myself, using the research they supplied. I learned the hard way. If only I'd actually talked to some of the people they'd worked with before me, instead of saying "My, what an impressive list of customers" and then asking for the outline, I would have saved myself time and the company money. I had forgotten that in a word-of-mouth niche business, you learn important things by seeking out word of mouth.

The other thing you can expect from your freelance writer is confidentiality and exclusivity. It is not uncommon, and it makes perfect sense, to insist on a signed confidentiality clause, especially if the preparation of a speech will entail the writer getting access to any commercially sensitive data. It simply makes sense, as well, that the writer you engage not be working for your competitor as well. No writer I know would willingly reveal to one client information learned from another. But mistakes do happen. So why not be clear and avoid any chance of loose lips.

Finally, of course, there is cost. This can vary widely from writer to writer and indeed between writers of equal seniority in different parts of the country. It's not unusual, however, in major metropolitan areas, to have senior writers with long CVs command in the neighborhood of $200+ an hour, with a major speech taking 20 or more hours to prepare. The time to prepare depends not so much on the writing but more on the amount of research to be done, not only on the organization but also on the sector and the overall business climate. Clearly, the more times you use a particular writer, the less time she will have to spend researching your company or your sector. But things change quickly in this world, and updating one's self on a number of clients in different sectors can be a time-consuming and therefore costly business.

Some writers, rather than charging by the hour, will quote on a project basis. This is a good way for you, as the buyer, to control costs. But depending on the pickiness of the client, it's not necessarily the way a freelancer will prefer to go. I had one client who was notorious for making changes, and always late at night. Eventually, I began quoting him very high estimates, just to be on the safe side. But the hours worked always exceeded even my most aggressive guesses for the total project cost.

That raises an important point about estimates. Certainly you should feel free to ask a seasoned pro to give you an estimate for a given project, whether by hours or an all-in cost. That said, often complications arise during the preparation of a speech that will drive the cost up. And to be fair, a large organization can often afford to eat the extra cost better than a one-person writing shop. That's especially true because in my experience most complications have their genesis in the organization. I have had occasions when we rewrote an entire speech because material circumstances had changed dramatically between draft 5 and draft 8.

Speechwriting is not like stamping out widgets. It's a dynamic, iterative process. I have had clients tell me what they want to say in some detail and then reject the draft once I give it to them. It's not that I got it wrong. I was, after all, a journalist who knew how to report a story told to me by contacts with some accuracy. Rather, it was the fact that once the speaker saw the words in black and white, he or she realized it wasn't quite, or even close to, what she wanted to say.

Access and Openness

Given that speechmaking is an iterative process, it follows that if there are things you can expect from a writer, there are also things the writer can expect from you.

Essentially, there are three: access, openness, and a willing-ness to pay on time.

There should be no question about the first two. A speech is a very personal thing. For a writer to work well, she has to get per-sonal with the speaker. And that means having access. At the very least that should mean a couple of meetings: one just as the process starts, to get a feel for where your head is at and the kind of points you want to make in a general way. Another meeting is useful after the first draft is submitted. Again, this enables you to get your response across directly to the writer, and it lets the writer probe (in a nice way, of course) to be clear about your reac-tions and how to fix the first draft. This kind of one-on-one ses-sion, especially if there's also an inside PR person present, can really shorten the cycle by clarifying fuzzy areas and new direc-tions.

There is also a strong argument to be made to allow the writer access to you in other settings—team meetings come to mind as somewhere the writer can hear the cadences of your speaking style and understand the kind of words you use. Bill Clinton used to tell his speechwriters he wanted his texts to sound as if he were talking to friends in his living room, and he ruthlessly excised any highfalutin language or rhetorical tricks. His writers wouldn't have been able to capture his unique phraseology if they hadn't had access to him.

But access applies to more than just the speaker. It also means opening the door for the writer to talk to others in the company, and get critical information. It's the rare CEO who has all the right data in his head at any given time, although I have known one or two who come pretty close. Rather, the meat of the speech will come from information supplied by the subject matter experts, in interviews, in combing through reports and presentations they've made, in finding the seed amidst all the chaff of the normal harvest of corporate information. Especially for a new writer, it's reasonable for him or her to ask for you or your lieutenant to give a heads-up to the subject matter experts so they are not blind-sided by a request for mission-critical confidential information from a stranger who doesn't even have a company e-mail address.

For the conjoined twin of access is openness. If you're going to be with the writer, it pays to be candid with her. This is not an adversarial relationship. This person will not run to the media with a scoop about disappointing earnings or to confirm (or start) rumors of layoffs. This is a person who is there to make you look brilliant and memorable on stage. Your personal brand and that of your company are on the podium with you, and to a certain extent, at least, in the hands and fertile imagination of your writer. Anybody can put 3,000 words together—well, not anybody, but a lot of people. What you want your writer to do is use her wit and skill and creativity to lift you above the ordinary. But she needs your help. And there's no telling what form that might take.

I remember once having a conversation with an executive, whining that I had so much work to do that I hadn't gotten around to do the research for a talk he had coming up in a few months. There was no panic, but this man liked to be ready, well in advance. At any rate, he asked me why I didn't just hire someone to do the research.

I said I would, but I didn't. Because when I research I really don't know what I'm looking for when I start out. Oh, I know the broad parameters. I know I want such and such data. But what I don't know is where I'll find that one inspirational spark that will make the connection with the audience, that will make the speech. It's like doing an Internet search. You'll type in your keywords and follow a link or two. Then all of a sudden, a link will come up that doesn't seem connected but it catches your eye. You follow it and take maybe a couple of other leaps of faith and, Eureka!, you've put two and two together in a totally new way. It happens more often than not.

That's why, as a writer, I have always craved openness from my clients. If they get to talking, just talking, one never knows what little tidbit of information will come out that will bring the high and mighty rhetoric down to a manageable, human level. Case in point: I was shooting the breeze with a client one day about family car trips. My family and I had just done a 24-hour straight run from Detroit to Tampa. He one-upped me, saying he used to take the family from Montreal to California, by car, in a week. Let me clarify that: The round trip was a week—two straight days on the road to get there, three days in the sun and then two days for the return trip. Loadsa fun! I filed it away and eventually used it in a speech about nothing being too tough if you really wanted it.

Openness speaks to the human connection. And it is a foundation for credibility. When you open the kimono, as they used to say when Japanese business methods were all the rage, people are going to believe you—because they can see you're not hiding anything.

The third essential point of expectancy for a writer is when he or she gets paid. This'll be short because it's a simple point. Many companies make it a policy to pay their suppliers only at the 60-day mark. This may be all right for suppliers who have a steady cash flow. But speechwriting is a cyclical business. Heavy in the fall and spring, dead around Christmas and in the summer. It's also predominantly a single proprietor–type business. Cash flow is an issue. And to wait two months to be paid for a service seems a bit over the top. I sometimes wonder what my cable company would say if I refused to pay until 60 days had elapsed since their bill was sent. But I guess I'll just continue to wonder. I love TV too much to test it.

Whose Words Are These? I Think I Know. The Speaker's. Not the Writer's.

White House speechwriters have gained some prominence in this generation, probably starting with Peggy Noonan. But people who write for business leaders continue to toil in almost total anonymity. And that is only right. For in the end, the words that come out of the speaker's mouth on the podium belong to no one but the speaker. It is he or she who said them publicly, after all. It is he or she who will have to live with any consequences of having said them.

Good speechwriters know that. They understand the fiction that lets audiences believe these leaders actually spend all that time crafting great lines and looking up quotations and supporting facts and figures themselves. The rush for them comes from seeing an audience respond as they anticipated. And in cashing the check.

It's something to keep in mind when dealing with writers, especially freelancers. The keyboard is not a place for prima donnas. The only spotlight, in the end, is on the speaker.

A Process that Works for Both

There is no right way and no wrong way to write a speech. Only a mutually beneficial way, one that works for both the writer and the speaker. At minimum, you should expect to have a meeting of some sort to rough out the opportunity and indicate some direction you might like to take. The writer then goes away to do some research and comes back with a draft. You respond, the writer fixes, you circulate for approvals and other input, the writer fixes again, and so on and so on.

One thing to note: I did not specify that the writer would initially come up with an outline to be approved. There's a reason for that. Even though clients often ask for an outline immediately after a first meeting, I always resist. The outline, if there is to be one, is part of the writing process. It is not part of the research and thinking process, which always comes first.

After an initial meeting with the client, my practice is to do all sorts of research, in a variety of directions, some clearly on topic and others less so, as I search for something that might key an organizing idea that will connect with the audience and make the speech memorable. It's only then that I feel I can write an outline that will accurately reflect the speech, an outline that hits not only on the data but also, and more significantly, on the tenor, tone, and theme—on what the audience will actually remember. And at that point, the hours it would take me to write the outline would be put to better use just drafting the talk. It means the client gets a look at something that's a lot closer to what the final product will look like. And it means we haven't wasted time preparing stuff that is likely to be totally revamped as a result of the research.

So if you still think you want an outline, don't ask for it the day after you assign the writer. It won't help you, or the writer, get to where you want to go.

How About the ROI?

There is a cost to giving a great speech—and not just in frayed nerves and sleepless nights. Even if you write it yourself, or some salaried person in your organization ghosts it for no overtime pay, there are hard and soft costs that have to be factored into your decision to speak or not to speak.

Indirect costs are toughest to tally, but a major speech can be a major time sink. First, there is an opportunity cost since, while you're thinking about, preparing for, and delivering your talk, you can't be riding herd to make sure the accountants aren't confusing revenues with expenses. Second, if you're doing the research and writing yourself, figure on thirty to forty hours. Third, even with a writer doing the rest of the work, you can allot about half a day for briefings and review meetings, another half a day of work by yourself to make sure you've covered the bases you need to cover, plus a half day to rehearse the delivery, even if you just do it in front of the mirror and the dog. And we haven't even arrived at the venue yet. So you're up to nearly two days invested in the project before you travel to the site, schmooze, deliver the talk, and then head back to the hotel room or home at the end of the day.

If you hire a writer, especially one with the expertise you need to build your personal brand, don't be surprised to start at $3,000

265

to $4,000 for a twenty-minute speech, with no ceiling in sight. A stump speech—one you'll repeat regularly—could go for much more depending on your seniority, the writer's experience, and what kind of deal you can negotiate.

All in, then, a fairly run-of-the-mill speaking opportunity could easily cost ten grand. More if there's extensive travel involved. Now, in a multibillion-dollar budget, that is walking-around money. But it's still money that could be spent elsewhere, unless you're certain that making a speech on a topic at a time is crucial to your strategy. Just as important, the time you invest is time you'll never have again, so be sure this is the best way to spend it.

Ideally, the organizers will be prepared to help you amortize your investment by ensuring a topnotch in-room audience. The ball is also generally in their court when it comes to getting the media there to spread your words far beyond the four walls of the hotel ballroom. Make sure you know how the organizers plan to get the media to the event, and augment their plans with your own resources, if need be. It's quite possible, even likely, for instance, that you or your organization would have some media contacts that might not be touched by the more general approach taken by the conference organizer. This is especially true among the vertical trade press, which in some industries is a powerful source of "what's what" and "who's who"; they tend to get short shrift from organizers more intent on gaining mainstream media attention.

Again, it's a question of protecting your own interests, which can get muted if the event organizers are left to their own devices. And by informing your contacts of your activities, even if they don't choose to cover the event, you have added one more brick to build that important relationship.

The same is true of your colleagues and bosses. It would improve your personal ROI immeasurably if the people who pull your strings saw you in a starring role. Is there an opportunity for this kind of personal lobbying in this invitation? Maybe not. The event may be in Hawaii while the people you're trying to impress are in Baton Rouge. But on the other hand, maybe so if it's in the hotel ballroom down the street. Again, no set answer, but an important question to ask before saying yes.

Index